ALL THE PAINTINGS OF
RAPHAEL
Part 1
VOLUME EIGHT
in the
Complete Library of World Art

The Complete Library of World Art

ALL THE PAINTINGS

OF RAPHAEL

Part 1

Edited by ETTORE CAMESASCA

Translated by LUIGI GROSSO

HAWTHORN BOOKS, INC.

Publishers · New York

Manufactured in Great Britain by Jarrold & Sons Ltd, Norwich

CONTENTS

RAPHAEL

Life and Work

RAPHAEL was still young, about thirty, when he achieved an almost legendary renown among his contemporaries; a reputation which, Michelangelo excepted, was unequalled in his time. This lofty regard still remains in his present reputation as a master painter, a fame perhaps greater than that of any other artist, ancient or modern. But is this opinion the fruit of real understanding? Has there ever been a full comprehension of Raphael, except by some of his contemporaries?

While Raphael's reputation as a man suffered somewhat by the almost inevitable comparison with Michelangelo, as an artist his reputation had already deteriorated by the middle of the sixteenth century by Tusco-Roman mannerists such as Vasari and others. Meanwhile, in Venice, Aretino and his followers, though ranking him above Michelangelo, proclaimed him inferior to Titian, thus starting a comparison which, like the previous and the following ones, has no true critical foundation. In Milan, Lomazzo considered him, together with six other companions, as one of the pillars of the idealistic temple of painting: elsewhere praise was given as a matter of course. The same thing was to occur in the seventeenth century when, though the object of general admiration, he was ranked with Carracci and Reni. He fared even worse at the hands of an author like Scannelli, who complained about the damaging effect the study of Raphael's works had on Bolognese academicians, while the Venetian Boschini stressed Titian's superiority even more categorically.

A more favorable criticism was that of the classicist Bellori, though he only granted Raphael "the good qualities of the ancients," including "grace." (In the following century, grace was to be personified by the work of Correggio.) The neo-classical movement of the late eighteenth century gave Raphael new prominence, but even this lasted only until Milizia formulated the pre-Raphaelite credo of discipline. When, later in the nineteenth century, art was conceived as "torment" or as "universal," not Raphael but Michelangelo and Leonardo represented the ideals to which people turned.

A true understanding of Raphael's art was finally achieved by the prophets of "pure vision." Yet, despite the enlightening pages of Wölfflin and others, how many convenient compromises were used before the present revaluation was reached! This, though convincing, remains confined to a rather small group of critics.

Born in 1483, Raphael may have learned the force of certain of Melozzo's rhythms from his father, Giovanni Santi, a competent painter (certainly the best in the Urbino of that time), who died when Raphael was only eleven. However, the boy must have drawn his initial artistic education, even outside the pictorial field, from masters other than his father. One can assume that the lucid proportions of the "crystal-architecture," conceived by Laurana for the Ducal Palace of the Montefeltro at Urbino, encouraged Raphael to think about the importance of balanced harmony of forms. For him this proved an introduction to an understanding of the qualities of light, space, and rhythm in the work of Piero della Francesca, in near-by Borgo San Sepolcro and in Urbino itself.

8

The earliest extant work by Raphael is the *Madonna and Child* frescoed in his father's home (*Frescos*, plate 1) and the *Standard* executed for the *Confratelli della Carità* in Città di Castello (plates 1 and 2). They show how Piero della Francesca bequeathed to him not only the characteristic features of his own figures, but also what was by now a conscious capacity for placing human figures, with a fine sense of balance and unity, within Flemish-inspired landscapes suggestive of those which the Dukes of Urbino were then collecting in large numbers. Meanwhile, from Perugia, Raphael had already felt the influence of Perugino, with whom he supposedly worked during the last years of the fifteenth century; and this is confirmed by the "rejuvenation," noted by Cavalcaselle, in the manner of Perugino from 1496 onwards. This favorable reverse influence is evidence of Raphael's precocious talent.

It is not surprising, therefore, that at the early age of seventeen he was entrusted—obviously following other commissions—with the painting of so important a work as an altarpiece representing the *Coronation of St Nicholas of Tolentino*. Nor are we surprised to find that in the contract the name of "Master" Raphael should precede that of his much older associate, Evangelista da Pian di Meleto. Moreover, while surviving fragments of this painting clearly show the contribution of both artists (plates 3 and 146A), a drawing preserved in Lille reveals that the underlying idea belonged to the latter. Raphael was already infusing the languid atmosphere of Perugino with some of the strong and vital character of the Florentine school. His form was derived from Leonardo da Vinci and Luca della Robbia—the latter's influence in Central Italy was widespread—and gives rise to Longhi's legitimate surmise that Raphael lived in Tuscany between 1496 and 1498.

In a short time (1500–2), Raphael also extended the range of his interests to the ornate incisiveness of Pinturicchio, consequently enriching the Perugino-like qualities of some small and lively works typified by the *Resurrection* of São Paulo (plate 4); but very soon, in 1502–3, the painter again approximated Perugino in the *Mond Crucifixion*, now in London (plate 10), and in the Vatican *Coronation* (plate 16), purposely divided into two autonomous areas. With its sense of spacious unity, an eloquent witness to useful contacts with Fra' Bartolomeo della Porta, the *Coronation* could hardly have been conceived after the London painting. The same discrepancy is shown by the steps of the two altarpieces. While the panels formerly beneath the *Crucifixion* (plates 14 and 15) reveal a truly Leonardesque fluidity, those still united with the *Coronation* (plate 17) appear rather rigid and inarticulate. In spite of this, it is the Vatican altarpiece more than the other that foreshadows the *Marriage of the Virgin* (Milan, Brera Gallery) where, however, Perugino's influence seems to have been translated in almost completely original terms.

The scheme of the panel in the Brera (plate 22) recalls that of the *Delivery of the Keys* in the Sistine Chapel and even more so the *Marriage* at Caen, both painted by Perugino. We are also reminded of his style by the over-emphasized sentimentality and the affected position of the most important figures. But the clever insertion of the temple within the arched section, the definite relation between architecture and figures and their inexhaustible series of interrelations, and the use of light to bring closer together the various parts of the painting: all these are eloquent testimony to the personal achievements of the twenty-year-old artist. It is therefore understandable that Raphael should have looked for an atmosphere more suited to his ambitions; yet his transfer to

Florence, in autumn 1504, probably was not the end of his connections with his native region. On his arrival, Raphael found two great artists at work: Leonardo da Vinci had already begun *Mona Lisa*, and was actively engaged on the project of *St Anne*: Michelangelo was finishing the *Doni Tondo*. Both artists were about to compete for the decoration of the Council Room of Palazzo Vecchio, for which they executed the famous cartoons of the *Battle of Anghiari* and the *Battle of Cascina*, now unfortunately lost. The Florentine painters of the time also included Lorenzo di Credi, Piero di Cosimo, Fra' Bartolomeo della Porta, and Perugino, who alternated his activities between Umbria and Tuscany. Some of these masters, as we have seen, were already known to Raphael, but there are reasons to believe that he was also interested in improving and extending his knowledge of the artistic achievements of Tuscany, going back as far as Masaccio, perhaps further, and from the field of painting into that of the sculpture of Donatello and others.

Conscious of the results he had already obtained and also, it seems, familiar with Florentine attainments, Raphael moved forward carefully in spite of many different influences. In the words of early historians, his sojourn in Florence was linked with "progress" in his artistic language towards a more fluid and unified artistic expression, that is, towards a greater "modernity." This is noticeable in the *Connestabile Madonna* (plate 31), in which the relationship between the figures in space produces an aesthetic tension unknown in his previous compositions involving this theme.

Equally, in the field of portraiture, the effective individualization learned from Perugino and further improved upon in such works as the Liechtenstein *Portrait of a Gentleman* (plate 21), the *Portrait of a Man* in the Borghese Gallery (plate 20), and the *Veiled Woman* in Hanover (plate 33), becomes more precious by new plastic and luminous means until it explodes into the brilliant and unrestrained explosion of color of the *Self-portrait* in Munich (plate 32).

Such luxuriance and freshness of enamels, particularly in relation to his subsequent methods of expression, was attributed by some to the influence of Francia. This is confirmed by a group of small panels in which pagan myth or Christian legend are made the pretext for enveloping nimble and rounded forms in an exhilarating, clear mountain atmosphere. Extreme care over formal values is the backbone of such small jewels, and candid, straightforward vision is subjected to disciplined organization.

The pure symmetry of the *Vision of a Knight*, in London (plate 44), still immature in spite of the masterly tree—inserted to center the lines of the composition round its foliage—generates an apt though unexpected *divertissement* by the introduction of the river in *The Three Graces* (plate 45); it is dissolved in the balancing elements of the *St Michael* (plate 46)—in which the cross on the shield carries the flashing movement from sword to leg; and it orders, with the help of the running figure at right, the dynamic vortex of the *St George* (plate 48), where the dragon's impetus is carried to an end, through the warrior's body, by means of the billowing cloak.

In 1505 Raphael returned to his native town in Perugia to continue the important works undertaken before his departure for Florence: the *Colonna Altarpiece*, now in New York (plate 37), for the nuns of St Anthony, and the *Ansidei Altarpiece*, now in London (plate 49), for the Church of San Fiorenzo. The former is dated about 1505 and the latter is inscribed 1506, but both must have been begun in 1503, as suggested by Cavalcaselle and confirmed by Longhi. According to Longhi, the London painting and what is left of its predella (plate 53) was the earlier of the two as indicated by its links with the old Umbrian manner, noticeable in spite of Raphael's efforts to conceal them under his Florentine style. The introduction of the rhythmic movement of the steps to the throne is also probably a result of Florentine influence: a superb idea, which finds no counterpart in the preparatory drawing in Frankfurt, and which, by repeating the motif of the arch above, increases the unity between the Saints at the sides. In the *Colonna Altarpiece*, the relation of the figures to their surroundings is a prelude to the spaciousness of the *Madonna of the Canopy*, while the accessory scenes (plates 39 and 40–1) reveal in their greater flow and coherence a deeper understanding of the stylistic laws of Leonardo da Vinci.

These laws, perceptible in terms of close agreement between form and feeling, had by now almost totally freed the artist from his ties with Perugino. This is shown in a series of Madonnas which began towards the end of 1504 with the *Granduca Madonna* in the Pitti (plate 42). The pensive figure of Mary, made even more monumental by the absence of any external embellishment, seems to evolve from the greenish darkness of the background (which has been painted over with a darker color), by a network of brush-strokes equally ready to break and melt into the mystery of diaphanous shadows, or to reveal more solidly the clear brilliance of forms, sculpturesque and yet weightless. In this succession of light and shade, the group seems lighted from within and the precarious balance of the two slightly diverging bodies (Wölfflin) is ultimately transformed into an unbreakable unity.

The progressive complexity of the elements of composition and their harmonious relationships while detracting from the perfection achieved in the loving mother and son permeated with religious feeling, nevertheless attains better formal solutions in other compositionally related paintings, such as the *Small Cowper Madonna* (plate 43), the *Northbrook Madonna* (plate 54), and the *Orléans Madonna* in Chantilly (plate 56). When the figure of the infant St John the Baptist is depicted, there follows a long series of variations on the pyramidal scheme, which become more and more rich stylistically, from the *Esterhazy Madonna* (plate 55), to the *Madonna of the Goldfinch* in the Uffizi (plate 63), and the *Madonna of the Meadows* in Vienna (plate 67). In the latter, the geometrical precision, which in the *Madonna of the Goldfinch* creates a quiet orderly pattern of curves gathered into an Olympian immobility, is eased in a first and more dynamic attempt to insert a smaller pyramid within the larger one. The main pyramid, composed of the figure of Mary, is used to join more firmly the figures of the two children forming the smaller pyramid and so achieve a closer compositional unity. There is undeniably a tension in this effort to enclose such contrasting spatial forces within an organized symmetry, but the discipline of Michelangelo (and perhaps also the restrained, classic taste of Luca della Robbia) was shortly to encourage Raphael to use more spontaneity in the control of such rhythms which seemed to be projected towards infinity.

The strong cohesion between the plastic and architectural quality of the human figures and the surrounding space which permeates them with light is already manifest in the *Virgin and Child with Beardless St Joseph* in Leningrad (plate 57) and in the *Holy Family with Palm* (plate 58) in London; one may consider it altogether achieved in the pious group of the *Canigiani Holy Family* in Munich (plate 77) in which, however, the monumental solemnity still implies an intellectual and somewhat visible effort; but it reaches its perfection in the exquisite restraint of *La Belle Jardinière* in the Louvre (plate 86). Here, Raphael's studies on the pyramidal pattern achieve a fine sense of unity between the figures, obtained by means of rounded planes within sinuous profiles and the ample rhythmical breath of the landscape under the light falling from the sky.

We thus come to the year 1507 which, judging by the Paris panel (plate 86), is thought to mark the conclusion of another direct attempt, following the example of Michelangelo, to confer permanence upon the vibrating elasticity of bodies caught in a moment of powerful contortion. At first Raphael finds a new means of expression (perhaps influenced by Pollaiuolo) by stressing the linear modulation as, for instance, in the *Holy Family with the Lamb* in Madrid (plate 83). But this device—which is already less evident in the *Bridgewater Madonna* (plate 84) and in the *Colonna Madonna*, Berlin (plate 85)—becomes a purely personal technique in the *St Catherine* in London (plate 89). In this work the formal research reaches its climax in the fascinating elliptic vortex of the symbolic wheel accentuated by the color sequence— red, yellow, blue-gray, green, then yellow and red again —and is further stressed by well-defined contours, by the placing of the hands, the serpentine folds of the robe, the angle of the head, and even by the *mise en scène* of landscape and clouds. If one notices further how this dynamic force is composed with a firm sense of unity, one is led to believe that Raphael has actually managed to solve the unprecedented problem of superimposing the vorticose movement of a tortile column upon the governing form of an obelisk.

Similar formal intentions are realized with freer atmospheric fusion in the *Casa Tempi Madonna* in Munich (plate 95), completed by 1508—which marked the end of Raphael's stay in Florence.

Meanwhile, in the field of portraiture, the transition from the *Portrait of Elisabetta Gonzaga* (plate 34), to *Emilia Pia of*

Montefeltro (plate 35) and to the *Young Man with an Apple* (plate 36) reveals how the rather dry individualization of the early Raphael when still influenced by Perugino, acquired in Tuscany a greater breadth and sense of color. This transition culminated in the pearly quality and spiritual atmosphere of the *Portrait of a Young Woman* in the Borghese Gallery (plate 61). Here da Vinci's example leads Raphael to achieve a kind of abstract blending with the surroundings which is less noticeable in the rich fullness of the *Doni* portraits (plates 68 and 70); these are hearty, more earthy—one is tempted to say—because of the massive superimposition of the figures on the landscape, in the strongly "realistic" manner of Ghirlandaio or Lorenzo di Credi.

After 1506 a combination of these numerous influences together with the first fruits of Venetian art reached Florence perhaps through Savoldo and Fra' Bartolomeo, who had returned from Venice in 1508. But this would only partly explain the stylistic substance of the *Pregnant Woman* in the Pitti (plate 71) and of the *Mute Woman* in Urbino (plate 93) which stand out from a dark background by means of extreme chiaroscuro that gives new resonance to the dense coloring. Indeed, that which is purely Raphaelesque in these architectonic portraits are to be found in the attention given the hands (so that the subtle interpretation of the faces and the geometric quality of the clothes should result in complete stylistic coherence) and in the miraculous transformation of such penetrating analysis into a supreme synthesis, forecasting the refined abstractions of Pontormo (Marangoni).

Although their far-reaching links with Mantegna, Signorelli, and the classic world are the most obvious, the *Pregnant Woman* and the *Mute Woman* reveal that Raphael had an extensive knowledge of the work of other artists. The Borghese *Deposition*, bearing the date MDVII, shows that

16

this knowledge had been assimilated to a greater extent. A comparison of the *Doni Tondo* by Michelangelo with the great panel in Rome (plates 72–3) is made inevitable by the powerful figures and is even obvious in the pious woman kneeling at right. However, while the punctilious preparatory work, documented by no less than sixteen drawings, in Florence, Paris, Oxford (plate 81), and elsewhere, reveals a multitude of sources, it shows how these external influences, which the artist considered compatible to, and even necessary for one another, were purified and resulted in Raphael's own expressive language. Conceived initially as a lament over the body of the dead Christ, the ultimate plan of the *Deposition* blends the theme of the entombment with that of the collapse of Mary; and the wedding of the two groups and of the various figures within each group, and finally between the figures and their surroundings, is achieved through a skilful web of interrelationships and dynamic spatial contrasts. Ultimately the resulting drama and pathos of the scene are exalted into an atmosphere of superhuman and typically Raphaelesque serenity. This work is not, therefore, the product of a cold and carefully calculated virtuosity, as some critics have even recently maintained, but rather of a lyrical, persuasive, and touching emotion which "embraces every part of this vital and tense web" (Ragghianti) and extends itself also to the *Christian Virtues* in the predella (plates 82A, B, and C). For the latter, the artist does away with the festive polychromy of the traditional steps, and using only monochromes, composes severe groups in the style of Michelangelo, immersing them in delicate blue tones, reminiscent of da Vinci's mysterious background.

In a letter of May 16, 1507, Raphael is called by Bembo a "great master of painting": this description makes the assumption even more plausible that he then possessed a workshop in Perugia which he shared with Berto di Giovanni and Domenico Alfani. There are documents to prove that on the following September 11, he was in Urbino. He had probably left Florence, not so much to revisit his native city, as to go to Perugia to complete, perhaps with the assistance of others, the fresco of the *Trinity and Saints* in the Church of the Monastery of San Severo, Perugia, which he began in 1505 when under the spell of the majestic spaciousness of Fra' Bartolomeo (*Frescos*, plate 2). This trend is more clearly marked in the *Madonna of the Canopy* in the Pitti (plate 91), presumably begun in 1507. Badly damaged, like the fresco, the Florentine altarpiece does not easily lend itself to interpretation because of work in it by Raphael's followers. However, we are not prevented, in spite of the magniloquence of the figures, from enjoying the artist's fine feeling for atmosphere, for example, in the definition of the space behind the throne.

Together with other works which were among those being executed in Florence at that period, according to Vasari, and which cannot be identified precisely, this was left unfinished because of Raphael's sudden departure for Rome. We do not know exactly when he departed, nor does his letter of September 5, 1508, sent from Rome to Francia, even if we accept its authenticity, constitute a sure limit *ante quem*. Even the reasons for his departure are not clear. Vasari claims that the Pope summoned Raphael to Rome at Bramante's suggestion, to work on the Vatican frescos. According to Vasari, Bramante was distantly related to Raphael, but we have no proof of this.

It is a fact, however, that, having given up the apartments of Alexander VI where the Borgian emblems, included by Pinturicchio in his decorations, recalled the unhappy memory of his predecessor, Pope Julius II chose his own new suite of chambers. He had already engaged several famous artists, including Sodoma and Bramantino, for this purpose. On his arrival in Rome, Raphael found some parts of the fresco cycles already begun. He commenced working on them himself (records of a payment to him on January 13, 1509, seem to refer to the Vatican frescos) and indeed with such success that after a short time he was left in sole charge of the work. By 1511 the decoration of the first *Stanza* (chamber), later known as *della Segnatura*, was completed: the vault, the *Disputa*, the *School of Athens*, the *Parnassus*, the *Virtues*, and other smaller parts.

With this achievement Raphael had enriched the cultural heritage of humanity with some of its finest masterpieces. The majestic polyphony of the *Disputa*, in particular, with its disciplined and rhythmic definition of space, the heroic intensity of its concept of modeling and chiaroscuro, and the lyrical use of light, are to be placed by unanimous consent among the greatest achievements in any field of art.

The vitality of the youthful limbs of the Vatican *Virtues* finds a counterpart in the *Aldobrandini Madonna* (plate 96) and an even worthier one in the *Alba Madonna* (plate 97), where the enveloping energy of the Michelangelesque profiles is modulated in diffused morning light. The same stylistic mood must have distinguished the *Madonna of the Veil* and the *Portrait of Julius II* painted for Santa Maria del Popolo in Rome, which are only known through indifferent copies now in Paris (plate 103A) and in Florence (plates 104 and 149B).

A direct echo of the prodigious solemnity in the first frescos of the *Stanza della Segnatura* is to be found in the *Foligno Madonna* (plate 100). Though leaving the Madonna in sublime isolation among the clouds, the composition nevertheless sets her in pious communion with the donor and the patron saints by means of a new development of the pyramidal scheme, repeated by the different postures of the main characters (connected in their turn by the *putto* (cherub) holding the plate). The composition in this painting was to become a law of *cinquecento* painting; in the same way those burning-bright colors were destined to exert a deep and lasting influence. Seldom, however, were the works which followed to achieve such a felicitous harmony of tones due, in this instance, to the prevalence of the range of grays which infuses a mysterious vitality into the vibrant brush-strokes in the background, reminiscent of Dossi.

The loss of the original *Portrait of Julius II* would be even more grave if we did not have the *Portrait of a Cardinal* in the Prado (plate 98) on which is based our knowledge of Raphael's portraiture during his first Roman period. Here, the ideal pyramid of so many previous compositions is doubled, but with an unexpected connection between the two favorite patterns, so that the top of the lower one, represented by the bust, is joined to the apex of the higher, which covers the pointed face under the red base of the cap. The abstract quality of such a scheme, while finding a valid ally in the bold sequence of colors, as clear and neat as enamels, stresses the hawk-like aloofness of the sharp aristocratic features.

After completing the fresco in one of the rooms of the Villa Farnesina depicting with festive and happy tones the pagan *Triumph of Galatea* (*Frescos*, plate 60) on which he worked between 1512 and 1514, Raphael undertook the decoration of another room in the Vatican, the *Stanza d'Eliodoro*, named after one of the scenes depicted on the walls (*The Expulsion of Heliodorus from the Temple*, in the same group as *The Mass of Bolsena*, *Leo I and Attila*, and the *Liberation of St Peter*). The diffused and crystal-clear transparency, which from his earliest works to the completion of the *Segnatura* had almost continuously created airy surroundings for his figures, is replaced now by a rather heavy, luminous texture. By fusing them into a more varied context of pictorial "accidents" Raphael perhaps provided an answer to the gigantic figures suggested by Michelangelo. The choice of light as a directive in the composition, agreeing perfectly with the Bramantesque sense of space which Raphael had substituted for the sometimes theatrical monumentality of Fra' Bartolomeo, runs parallel to an increasing Venetian influence. The Venetian influence was due to his rivalry with Sebastiano del Piombo, but more particularly to collaboration with Giovanni da Udine and, as Longhi rightly assumed, with Dossi and Lorenzo Lotto. It is also probable that the greater lightness and rapidity of this new taste was partly derived from a knowledge of the recently discovered Roman paintings of Greek descent, that Raphael had possibly acquired from works later destroyed. Better than in the *St Cecilia* of Bologna (plate 106), where its effect is rather uneven and ponderously contrived, the result of many influences is to be seen in the elaborate conception of some of his Madonnas: the *Madonna of the Fish* in Madrid (plate 108), the *Madonna dell'Impannata* in the Pitti (plate 109), the *Madonna of the Curtain* in Munich (plate 110), and the *Madonna of the Chair*, also in the Pitti (plate 111). In this last work, by an even more strictly compositive scheme, that is, by the perfect subordination to the circular panel emphasized by contrasting the small St John to the rotative movement of the other two figures, Raphael expressed his carefully controlled compositional sense, which in the previous Madonnas had led to a magnificent harmony of rhythmical modulations.

Raphael was by now overwhelmed by commitments; on April 1, 1514 he was appointed Architect of the Church of St Peter in Rome, as the assistant to Bramante who, dying shortly after, was replaced as director of the work on the Basilica (August 1), by his young colleague. Moreover, Raphael had for some time been devoting himself to archaeology and to the execution of a plan of ancient Rome. While he practised in the field of the plastic arts and studied the classics of architecture, he was entrusted with diverse duties ranging from plans for new buildings to projects for precious household goods and furnishings, from mosaics to tombs, prints to stage-settings, from mantelpieces and chimneys (and sometimes even their mechanics) to medals and coins. But at the same time commissions for portraits, altarpieces, and secular pictures continued. Furthermore, between each great cycle of frescos in the Vatican, Raphael executed minor compositions in the same medium. In the period between 1511 and 1514, he painted the *Isaiah* in the Roman Church of Sant'Agostino, the sybils in the Church of Santa Maria della Pace, and the already mentioned *The Triumph of Galatea* in the Villa Farnesina.

Such a formidable array completed in an amazingly short time makes it difficult to define the importance and chronological order of the various stylistic experiments even when —and this becomes progressively rarer—the still very high standard of workmanship points undeniably to Raphael's personal execution. Since it is easy to determine the more or less extensive contributions by his assistants in various works from the *St Cecilia* of Bologna onwards (the difficulty here is to distinguish between Giulio Romano, Penni, and many other helpers), the hand of the master himself remains easily recognizable in such paintings as the *Sistine Madonna* and certain portraits of the same period.

Executed for the monks of San Sisto at Piacenza, the *Sistine Madonna* (plate 116) confirms once again the genius of Raphael. Between the gentle folds of the right-hand curtain and the broad curvature of Mary's mantle falling from the flexed arm of the Child (and continued by the line which ends below the female Saint); between the sinuous flowing of the sacerdotal vestments of St Sixtus and the curving veil of the Madonna; between every element we find a continuous echo of forms in an atmosphere of supreme harmony. Despite a certain coldness in the colors softened by the silvery light of the clouds, this harmony pervades the whole composition.

Among the portraits of the same period, one should note the valid one of Pope Julius II, whose features are those of the saint of the *Sistine Madonna* (plate 118). Of greater importance are the *Fedra Inghirami* in Boston (plate 112), duplicated later in the Florentine painting of the same composition (plate 113), and the *Baldassar Castiglione* in Paris (plate 115). In the dense and enameled majesty of the first, the massive planes are modulated in a slow circular movement stressed also by the sitter's squint, which is therefore elevated to the rank of a stylistic norm. The static, dignified pose of Castiglione is relieved by a delicate and rich range of grays and enlivened by soft, silvery lights which create a magnificent link between the subtle expression of the face—accentuated by his leaning slightly forward—and the opulent fold of his dress. This portrait of Castiglione was said to be the most completely Renaissance representation produced in the whole period. And indeed it would be impossible for us to find another portrait in which the ideals of the period are embodied in an individual with such absolute and incomparable perfection.

Between 1514 and 1517 Raphael executed two cycles of frescos in the third *Stanza* (*Fire in the Borgo*, the *Battle of Ostia*, the *Coronation of Charlemagne*, and the *Oath of Leo III*) and those in the vaulted bathing room of Cardinal Bibbiena in the Vatican (*Frescos*, plate 107). These were followed, before the end of 1519, by frescos in the *Logge* and the *loggetta*, on the third floor of the Papal Palace (*Frescos*, plates 128–56) and by the other fresco in the *Loggia of Psyche* in the Villa Farnesina (*Frescos*, plates 108–27). At the same time the famous series of tapestries, based on the cartoons prepared under Raphael's supervision in approximately 1515 (plates 153–60), also destined for the Vatican, was being woven in Brussels; at this same time Raphael was also supervising construction work for Cardinal de' Medici on a villa, later called the Villa Madama.

After the frescos of the *Stanza dell'Incendio*, the critics usually notice a progressive decline, forecast by a regression in taste. Some lowering of quality is already visible in the *School of Athens*. Except for a few instances, this decline is continued right up to the complete decadence of Raphael's last works. His last period of activity, considered as the sum total of paintings bearing his name, appears less coherent than his first; after some initial lack of balance the inspiration drawn from Michelangelo loses freshness and sincerity until it becomes exterior and mechanical, and finally reaches the level of inert illustration; his fresh lyrical sense often becomes turgid oratory; in short, the transformation of the rivulet into a mighty river makes its once limpid waters rather muddy (Ortolani). However, the last five years of Raphael's life and the consequences of his ever-increasing intimacy with cultured Roman society, which was so deeply imbued with the art of ancient Rome, deserve a more profound study.

It is not coincidence that the papal brief appointing him Safekeeper of the Ancient Inscriptions of Rome bears the date 1515. The enthusiasm, indeed the courage with which Raphael undertook his new assignment, which manifests once more his passion for antiquity, assumes a special meaning if we compare it with the accompanying decline of his love for painting. And in fact, if he still appeared wholly engaged in his old profession, it was more as director of a society of artists than as a creative artist. Significantly, a sum of money for the execution of several works, once attributed to Raphael and now to his school, was paid to the "young men of Raphael"—his apprentices. These latter remained united in spite of their differences in temperament, and succeeded after his death in obtaining such commissions as, for instance, the decoration of the Vatican *Sala di Costantino*, even if they were aided by their claim that they possessed some of Raphael's drawings for the project. Not everything in this collaboration is clear. Raphael's contribution, however, was probably limited to a few sketchy suggestions in the preparatory stage and some sporadic assistance when the work was almost finished: and this is true of many paintings and frescos.

Are we perhaps to believe that in his last phase, deeply absorbed as he was in his architectural and archaeological studies and, conversely, so uninterested in the execution of the pictorial commissions undertaken in his workshop, that Raphael was approaching a radical change in his means of expression? Or could he possibly have been looking for a more complete means of self-expression, uniting all the possibilities of the various branches of art he had been cultivating? The completion of Villa Madama might perhaps have given us a decisive answer, but unfortunately the building was left unfinished, and its decoration undertaken several years after Raphael's death.

But leaving aside conjecture, let us follow Raphael's career when, after a sudden revival of his passion for painting (or because he had been affected by his rivals' gossip), he devoted greater energy and patience to the conception of a work or even went back to his brushes to complete the execution himself. It is then that masterpieces were created which, though often neglected or misunderstood by the critics, are absolutely essential for a full understanding of Raphael's genius.

The highest achievements of this last phase are the cartoons for the Vatican tapestries. Of the remaining seven (now in London), *Elymas struck with Blindness* (plate 156A) and *The Sacrifice at Lystra* (plate 158A) are superficial declamations which border on archeology and choreography. A majestic sense of order is clearer in *The Death of Ananias* (plate 157A) and in the rhythmic relations between architecture and figures in *The Preaching of St Paul* (plate 159A); in *The Miraculous Draught of Fishes* (plate 153A), the figures towering against the still background of the lake diffuse a warm feeling of life and religious solemnity into an abstract order reminiscent of a classic bas-relief.

In *The Delivery of the Keys* (plate 153B), although the cartoon is not entirely his own work, Raphael expressed one of the most sublime concepts in the whole of Italian painting. The conciseness and drama of the composition is obviously derived from the *Tribute* by Masaccio which he had presumably studied during the winter of 1515–16 in Florence, where he went to take part in the competition for a design for the façade of San Lorenzo and where he met Michelangelo and the chief Italian architects of the period. But Raphael brings to the subject an unprecedented departure in the "grand manner" of such unique sublimity that, by comparison, previous and contemporary trends, though they contributed to this new development, appear somewhat limited and decidedly polemic. By doing away with all reminders of personal expression and private circumstance

—and this is the real substance of *The Delivery of the Keys*, a gathering of men conceived as a simple and perfect colonnade—Raphael finally achieved the ideal of untroubled universality sought by the Humanists. Words cannot express the sense of pleasure, fulfilment, and the quietening of the senses in front of the supreme order created by the artist.

Returning to the beginning of Raphael's career, we must admit that no artist before him, with the exception of Masaccio, managed to cover so much distance in so short a time. The gentle and virginal dreamer of ten years earlier soon found a quiet, tranquil, and poetical mode of expression that was gradually to rise to a virile, heroic, and finally choral crescendo. This miraculous transformation was made possible by Raphael's innate genius for translating in terms of style any and all external elements. In addition, he had the capacity for penetrating the essence of the figurative languages of Italy, both present and past. From these heterogeneous and sometimes even contradictory premises, Raphael was able to achieve coherence and balance.

After his explorations in the field of Italian art, he delved into numerous streams of culture and his untiring passion for experiment drew him toward the monuments of the ancient classic world. In his last phase, in fact, he re-lived the plastic evolution of Rome. It is to the expression of such noble feeling, matured through a natural process, that we owe the ensuing expansion of forms in a seemingly monotonous structure. This phase is neither sterile immobility nor facile escape into mere illustration, nor is it the fruit of unusual eclecticism; and it is proved by the impossibility of defining these achievements within a comprehensive formula (which would have greatly facilitated an assessment of Raphael's artistic stature). The artist's last phase owes nothing to the attractive qualities of the subjects, nor to mistaken romantic ideals of originality, but on the contrary increases the poetic tension. This manner does neglect the skilful weaving of beautifully harmonized or opposed geometrical patterns, but only in order to envelop the perspective and spatial elements of composition with moving solemnity; it stifles every sensuous impulse in execution, but only to blend and harmonize with an intense and effective contemplative attitude. To sum up, it may be said that, freed of every desire to schematize, Raphael's mind, serene and powerful, enters the extremely civilized classic world, freeing the infinite lyrical grandeur contained therein and revealing, by means of a slow and coherent process, its inexhaustible values.

Referring to the other masterpieces of the last period some critics have used the words "proto-Baroque" and even more frequently "pre-Mannerism." Of course one can admit that Raphael was precociously sensitive to spiritual unease which became tragic in Michelangelo's case and was to become anguish in his successors. Raphael's purpose, interpreting reality with new means, is noticeable in some portraits painted after 1515. Leaving aside some works of doubtful authenticity, *La Velata* (plate 119), which one might almost call the "Portrait of a Sleeve," reveals a transference of interest towards a concept which, in its variety of forms, colors, and lights, is no longer plastic but may be considered a forerunner to the prolific work of the Venetian *settecento* (Marangoni). The very choice of models may in itself have imposed a more massive framework on the portrait of *Leo X and two Cardinals* (plate 128). This does not, however, detract from the serpent-like mobility to be found in the interplay of planes defining the figures, in the spacious circular movement of the rooms—the *girar delle stanze* (Vasari), emphasizing its Baroque character—and in the

28

wealth and exuberance of the enamel-like colors that transform space into "moulded light" (color plate VIII).

Pre-Manneristic accents in the execution of the outlines are present—we ignore those works in which the contribution of the school seems to have killed the original Raphaelesque idea—in the so-called *Spasimo di Sicilia* (plate 124), in the *St Michael and the Devil* of the Louvre (plate 129), and in some Holy Families, such as *La Perla* in Madrid (plate 132) and the two Paris works (plates 130 and 131). The extreme sensuousness in terms of space and color which distinguishes these works subsides into clarity of line in the *Vision of Ezechiel* (plate 125). This picture disregards previous compositional procedure, raising the eye of the beholder up to the level of the celestial group and relegating the main character to the distant bottom of the painting. A new and cruder expression of such sensuousness is found in *The Visitation* in Madrid (plate 137), where the constantly changing colors—not necessarily due to Penni's contribution—helps to determine the abstract intellectual quality of the whole.

At the same time we notice a foretaste of strong preCaravaggesque realism which was to find a more impressive expression in the group of Apostles on the left of the Vatican *Transfiguration* (plate 140). The dramatic vortex is dominant in the upper part of the painting (plate 142) and is articulated according to extremely coherent linear and plastic laws. The figures tremble under the impact of the light, which seems to melt away their soft colors and absorb their outlines. In the lower part of the composition, however, the light is very strong, accentuating the striking and bustling activity of the group of figures on the right. This difference between upper and lower sections was criticized as early as the eighteenth century by de Brosses, in spite of the fact that in that period the panel was described as "the most beautiful in the world." And indeed, this dualism cannot be justified on the grounds of the different natures, divine and human, of the two sharply different areas. The responsibility for this mistake is not, however, Raphael's. He died, after a short illness, on April 6, 1520, while the painting was still unfinished. The *Transfiguration* was later completed by Giulio Romano and Penni, whose extensive contributions to this work is proved by the huge sum paid them for their work.

The *Transfiguration* was exhibited over Raphael's bier in all its unfinished beauty, and all who came realized the exceptional stature of the artist who had died at the early age of thirty-seven, and who was considered by all who knew him as the best of men.

BIOGRAPHICAL NOTES

1483, APRIL 6. Raphael born in Urbino "at three o'clock of the night" (Vasari) to the painter Giovanni di Sante di Piero (a descendant of a Sante who had lived at the beginning of the fourteenth century, hence the patronymic "Santi") and to Magia di Battista di Nicola Ciarla, his wife.

1491, OCTOBER 7. Raphael's mother dies.

1494, AUGUST 1. His father, who had remarried on May 25, 1492, dies.

1500. According to a legal document dated May 13, Raphael has left Urbino. On December 10, together with Evangelista da Pian di Meleto, he begins painting the *Coronation of St Nicholas of Tolentino* for the Andrea Baronci chapel in the Church of Sant'Agostino in Città di Castello.

1501, SEPTEMBER 13. The above-mentioned altarpiece is known to be completed.

1501–3. During this period the Abbess of the Monteluce Convent of the Order of St Clare in Perugia commissions him to do the *Coronation of the Virgin*, which was executed after Raphael's death by his pupils. The date, MDIII, was noted by Margherini Graziani (*L'arte a Città di Castello*, Città di Castello, 1897) in an inscription on

the *Mond Crucifixion* now in London.

1504. Date inscribed on the *Marriage of the Virgin*, now in Milan. A letter of October 1 (considered false or not even relating to Raphael by some critics) written by Giovanna Feltria, wife of Giovanni della Rovere, recommends Raphael to the Gonfaloniere Soderini before the artist moved to Florence.

1505. Date inscribed under the fresco in the Church of San Severo in Perugia, considered by some critics false or too late; the same date was inscribed on the *Madonna of the Meadows*, now in Vienna. Other documents referring to the *Coronation* in Monteluce are dated December.

1506. The date, MDVI, was seen on the *Ansidei Altarpiece*, now in London.

1507. Date of the *Deposition*, now in Rome; the same date possibly appears on *La Belle Jardinière*, now in Paris, and on the *Holy Family with the Lamb*, now in Madrid. The *Prayer in the Garden*, now lost, was probably finished in this year (see page 97). On October 11, Raphael is known to be in Urbino.

1508. Date of the *Large Cowper Madonna*, now in Washington. On April 21, he writes from Florence to his uncle, Simone Ciarla.

31

Malvasia (*Felsina pittrice*, Bologna, 1678) published another letter which Raphael is supposed to have written on September 5 in Rome to Francesco Francia, but this is now rightly considered false.

1509. The first proof of his stay in Rome appears in a document of January 13. On October 4, he is appointed as a Writer of Pontifical Briefs.

1510. Papers mention his relations with the goldsmith Rossetti, a goldsmith of Perugia.

1511. Date inscribed under the *Parnassus* and *Virtues* in the Vatican *Stanza della Segnatura*. In November he puts up bail for the painter, Baldassarre Peruzzi.

1512. Date inscribed under the *Mass of Bolsena* in the *Stanza d'Eliodoro*. During the same year he works, perhaps, on a portrait of Federico Gonzaga, now lost.

1513, JULY 7. He receives 50 ducats from the Treasurer of Leo X presumably for resumption of work on the *Stanze*.

1514. Elena, wife of Benedetto dall'Olio, commissions the *St Cecilia* in Bologna. On April 1, he is appointed Architect to the Church of St Peter, as assistant to Bramante, from whom he takes over as director of the work on August 1. Presumably in June, he completes the *Stanza d'Eliodoro*. On July 1, he writes to his uncle, Simone; on August 15, to Marco Fabio Calvo (some consider this letter a forgery) and around the same period, to Castiglione.

1515. In a letter (June 7) written by Agostino Gonzaga to Isabella d'Este, in a second letter (November 8) from Castiglione to the same, and in a third (November 30) from the Marchesa to Castiglione, there are allusions to a "small painting" that Isabella wanted to obtain from Raphael (it is mentioned again in another letter, perhaps of 1519, written by Paolucci to the Duke of Ferrara). The first hint of the cartoons for the Vatican tapestries is found in a receipt dated June 15. A document entrusting Raphael as Safekeeper of the Ancient Inscriptions of Rome is dated August 27. On November 8 he is presumably in Florence, called there together with the greatest architects of Italy to discuss plans for the façade of the Church of San Lorenzo.

1516. Date on the mosaics in the Chigi Chapel of Santa Maria del Popolo in Rome, executed by De Pace from drawings by Sanzio. On April 3, Bembo writes to Bibbiena announcing that on the following day Raphael intended to go on an archeological outing to Tivoli, together with Castiglione, Navagero, Beazzano, and Bembo himself. In another letter to Bibbiena (April 19), Bembo speaks of the portrait of Castiglione, now in Paris, as already completed, the one of "Our Duke" (variously identified), and the lost portrait of Tebaldeo. In a legal document of May 23, Raphael is mentioned as being owed more than 1,000 florins by Valerio Porcari, perhaps for paintings or architectural work. On June 20, Bembo tells Bibbiena of the completion of the decorations in the

Cardinal's bathing room in the Vatican. On June 21, the contract for the *Coronation* of Monteluce is renewed. On July 7, Benedetto Capilupi writes to Isabella d'Este suggesting she acquire some silver bowls designed by Raphael. On November 22, Leonardo Sellaio writes to Michelangelo about a small *putto* (cherub) modelled in clay by Raphael and sculpted in marble by Pietro d'Ancona. On December 20, the sum still owed him for the execution of the cartoons for the Vatican tapestries was paid.

1517. Date of two sonnets by Castiglione on a portrait of a lady painted by Raphael. On January 19, writing to Michelangelo, Leonardo Sellaio alludes to the *Transfiguration*, now in Rome, and to Raphael's disappointment at finding himself competing with Sebastiano del Piombo. Between March 21 and December 4, Ambassador Constabili writes to the Duke of Ferrara about a *Triumph of Bacchus* that Raphael should have painted for the Duke. From one of these letters (June 6), we learn that the *Stanza dell'Incendio* is nearly completed, and it was in fact finished by the beginning of July. On July 1, a payment was made to Raphael's pupils for certain decorations executed in the Vatican (possibly in the *Sala dei Palafrenieri*). Writing to Michelangelo on September 26, Sellaio says that Raphael is working on the *Transfiguration*. In November, Raphael sends the cartoon for the *Battle of Ostia* to the Duke of Ferrara. On November 6, Lorenzo de' Medici, Duke of Urbino, expresses the intention of asking Raphael to design some coins for him.

1518. Sellaio tells Michelangelo (January 1) of the completion of the *Loggia of Psyche* in Villa Farnesina. In some letters between January 22 and February 5, the *Portrait of Lorenzo de' Medici* (plate 144) is mentioned as already executed. Between March 1 and June 19, letters by various writers allude to the *St Michael and the Devil* and to the *Holy Family of Francis I*, both in Paris, and finished, as is known, on May 27. On April 21, a payment is made which is probably connected with the transportation of the Vatican tapestries from Flanders to Italy. On July 2, writing to Michelangelo, Sebastiano del Piombo says that Raphael has not yet begun the *Transfiguration*. On July 11, perhaps by virtue of his authority as a keeper of Roman remains, Raphael claims one or more statues left by a certain Gabriele de' Rossi. On August 13, on the subject of the still unfinished *Triumph of Bacchus*, Ambassador Constabili alludes to Raphael's intense activity as an architect and painter. Between September 21 and November 20, there is another intensive exchange of letters between the Court of the Este and Constabili on the *Triumph of Bacchus*; on November 10, the cartoon of the *St Michael* arrives in Ferrara, sent as a gift by the master; previously (September 22), Constabili himself had given to a pupil of Sanzio (Battista Dossi?) a letter of introduction to Duke Alfonso. Between December 29 and March 2, 1519, there is a new exchange of letters about the *Triumph*; Raphael sends to the Court of Ferrara the cartoon for the *Portrait of Giovanna d' Aragona*, now in Paris.

After 1518? Raphael and Antonio da Sangallo the Young study some works of town planning in Rome in their capacity as "masters of the roads."

1519. Raphael sends the well-known letter to Leo X (written by Castiglione) on the subject of the map of ancient Rome which he was then preparing. In two letters (March) from the Ambassadors of the Este family in Rome, there are allusions to the scenery conceived by Sanzio for the comedy *I Suppositi*, by Ariosto. Between April 30 and September 2 there is another intensive exchange of letters concerning the often-mentioned *Triumph*. On May 7, Raphael receives 400 ducats in payment of work for the Pontifical Court. On June 3, writing to Federico Gonzaga, Castiglione refers to the drawing of a tomb executed by Raphael. For the Christmas season, seven tapestries of the series by Raphael are exhibited in the Sistine Chapel.

1520. During the period between January 20 and March 21, there is another exchange of letters between the Ambassador of Ferrara and his Court on the subject of the *Triumph*; in one of them (March 20), it appears that Raphael had promised to make the drawings for some fireplaces for Alfonso I. On April 6 Raphael dies, three hours after the Angelus, "of a continuous and acute fever which he had had for eight days," according to the testimony of Paolucci the Estense Ambassador. Although not very detailed, his account is nevertheless more dependable than the information given by Fornari and Vasari, who tend to connect the death of the master with erotic excesses.

RAPHAEL'S PAINTINGS

Plate 1

CRUCIFIXION. *Canvas, 112 × 66.**
*Città di Castello, Pinacoteca Comu-
nale.* One of the two sides of the
Standard painted for the *Confratelli
della Carità* in Città di Castello which
are kept today in the Misericordia
Hospital. Mancini (*Istruzione. . . , di
Città di Castello*, Perugia, 1832) attributed it to the School of Perugino;
ascribed by Guardabassi (*Indiceguida
dei nonumenti nell'Umbria*, Perugia,
1882) to Francesco da Castello; now
exhibited as "Umbrian School of the
sixteenth century." Longhi had
already begun attributing it to
Raphael in 1922, writing about it
in *Piero della Francesca* (Milan, 1927),
and recently (in 1955) confirmed the
attribution, of which there is no
trace except in Ragghianti (1947),
and in the catalogue of the Florentine
exhibition, "The Italian House
through the Centuries" (1948).
Longhi, stressing the links with
Perugino's altarpiece at Fano, in
addition to the signs of Della
Francesca's influence, dates it around
the last years of the fifteenth century.
The work is in a bad state of
preservation, very worn and partly
repainted.

Plate 2

THE MADONNA OF THE MISERI-
CORDIA. *Canvas, 112 × 66. Città
di Castello,* cf. above. Together with
the above painting (see plate 1) this
work formed the *Standard* executed
for the *Confratelli della Carità* in

Città di Castello. Longhi notes the
strong influence of Piero della
Francesca mixed with more recent
suggestions of Perugino and Flemish
sources (in the landscape), and the
affinities with the fresco painted
shortly before in Raphael's own
home at Urbino (*Frescos*, plate 1).
The portraits of the brothers, on the
left, have been largely repainted; the
portraits of their wives on the right-
hand side of the painting are better
preserved.

Plate 3

ANGEL. *Panel, 31 × 27. Brescia,
Pinacoteca Tosio Martinengo.* Frag-
ment of the altarpiece representing
the coronation of St Nicholas of
Tolentino, the execution of which
was entrusted to Raphael and
Evangelista da Pian di Meleto on
December 10, 1500, for the Church
of Sant'Agostino in Città di Castello.
Completed on September 13, 1501,
the painting was damaged in an
earthquake in 1789. In the same year,
Pius VI acquired what was left of it.
Some small fragments were kept in
the Vatican up to the time of the
Siege of Rome in 1849, when they
were dispersed. The existing painting
was in the collection of Count Tosio
in Brescia, from which it passed to
its present home. A free copy of the
original work, perhaps made in the
seventeenth century, once kept in
the Convent of the Augustinian
Sisters in Città di Castello and now
to be found in the local gallery, and

* All dimensions are given as centimeters.

a drawing in Lille, allow one to establish what comprised the lost altarpiece: top center, God holding a crown among various cherubs; at left, Mary holds out a crown (plate 146A); at right, St Augustine; below, Nicholas's feet rest on Satan; at left, an angel, and to the right another two angels (one of whom forms the extant work) hold scrolls with inscriptions on them; in the background, a large arch through which a landscape can be seen. The altarpiece was very big, perhaps the largest ever painted by Raphael on panel before the Vatican *Transfiguration*. The recognition of this and of the Naples fragments is due to Fischel (*Jahrbuch der preussischen Kunstsammlungen*, 1912)—previously this work was attributed to Timoteo Viti—but cleaning executed by Cavenaghi (1912) made the identification positive.

Plate 4

RESURRECTION. *Panel, 52 × 44. São Paulo, Brazil, Art Museum.* Discovered by Böde in 1857 in the Kinnaird Collection at Rossie Priory (Perthshire) who brought it to the attention of Cavalcaselle. The latter mentions it without passing any judgment. In 1927, Regteren van Altena established the relationship between this work and the two drawings by Raphael kept in Oxford, usually linked with the *Resurrection* commissioned from Perugino in 1499, and kept today in the Vatican (see page 114). This work remained in the London market for several years, as a painting by a pupil of Perugino; the attribution was Berenson's. Suida identified it as the painting mentioned by Cavalcaselle, and dated it 1503. Ragghianti (*Selearte*, 1954) considers it one of Raphael's "very first panels", its period close to the *Baglioni Annuncia-*

tion in Perugia"; according to Longhi (1955), it belongs to the phase of Pinturicchio's influence, that is, in the period 1501–2. On the other hand, many critics exclude it from the body of works by Raphael, preferring to see in it the work of Perugino or of some of his followers, such as Viti or Eusebio da San Giorgio. The work reveals traces of restoration.

Plate 5

ST SEBASTIAN. *Panel, 43 × 34. Bergamo, Accademia Carrara.* In the possession of the Zurla family at Crema, this panel was then bought for 3,000 liras by the well-known engraver Giuseppe Longhi who sold it in 1836 to Lochis. Unanimously attributed to Raphael, the work is considered to have been painted in the period of Perugino's influence. Chronologically, however, the work is very controversial: about 1501 for Ortolani; about 1502 for Fischel and Gamba; 1503 according to A. Venturi; 1503–4 according to Pittaluga; 1503–5 for Gronau, Gnoli, and Ottino della Chiesa (*Accademia Carrara*, Bergamo, 1955). The importance of elements drawn from Pinturicchio leads one to agree with Longhi (1955) upon the earliest date, 1501–2.

Plate 6

THE SOLLY MADONNA. *Panel, 52 × 38. Berlin, Staatliche Museen.* Mary's cloak is blue, with a red lining and the book is black and gold. The Child grasps a piece of string in his right fist, with which he holds the little finch in his left hand. The painting came to its present location in 1821 from the Solly Collection. Unanimously attributed to Raphael. Gronau dates it about 1502, A. Venturi as 1502–3, Pittaluga as 1503–4. Gamba, together with Fischel, dates it earlier—in

1500, and Ortolani suggests about 1501. Abrasions and traces of cleaning are noticeable, and it is probable that this has been the main reason why the colors have faded. Longhi (*Paragone*, 1952) reproduces an important copy, now in an Italian private collection, which he considers authentic and probably painted a few months before the Berlin version.

Plate 7

MADONNA WITH CHILD AND SS JEROME AND FRANCIS. *Panel, 34 × 29. Berlin, Staatliche Museen.* The two churches in the background are meant to represent the missions of the two Saints. Previously in the Borghese Collection, the panel was sold in 1829 to the King of Prussia; it is unanimously attributed to Raphael. Fischel dates it as 1500; Ortolani as 1501; Rosenberg and Gronau as around 1502; A. Venturi as 1502–3; and Pittaluga as 1503–4. Cavalcaselle lays emphasis on the influence of Perugino, together with some of Pinturicchio. Gamba, dating it 1499, believes it was based on a drawing by Pinturicchio himself. Longhi (1955), though agreeing with Gamba, places it in the phase of Pinturicchio's influence (about 1502). Much restored, particularly on the right-hand side, the panel was very likely submitted to excessive cleaning which resulted among other things, in the obliteration of the names of the Saints inscribed in the halos. Longhi (*Paragone*, 1952) mentions an autograph copy of a rather later date which passed from the Grassi Collection to the Warburg Collection in New York.

Plate 8A

CRUCIFIX WITH SAINTS. *Small astel-crucifix with two faces. Rome.* Formerly the property of Marchese Emilio Visconti Venosta and transferred to Rome. Inside the circles within the trilobes, Mary and St John are seen against a red background, at the sides of the crucifix; at the top St Peter with the Keys, beneath Mary Magdalen holding a vase containing perfumes. Ricci (*Pinturicchio*, London, 1902; Paris, 1903; and Perugia, 1915) believed it to be by Pinturicchio and dated it as 1497–1500; Gamba also attributes it to Pinturicchio (*Dedalo*, 1920–1), admitting that Raphael may have co-operated. Volpe considers it undoubtedly Raphael's work (*Paragone*, 1956) and dates it as 1501–2.

Plate 8B

CRUCIFIX WITH SAINTS, reverse side of the crucifix. The saints represented are Francis and Claire at the sides of the crucifix; Louis of Toulouse at the top and Anthony of Padua at the bottom.

Plate 9A

THE TRINITY WITH SS SEBASTIAN AND ROCHE. *Canvas, 166 × 94. Città di Castello, Pinacoteca Comunale.* Previously a standard which was already so damaged by 1638 that it had to be dismantled. After this, the two original paintings were lodged in the Church of the Trinity at Città di Castello, for which it had been painted. Together with its twin it was deposited with Count Della Porta (1867–8) who undertook the restoration. After removing the dirty crusts and the repaintings (executed by Caratoli, among others) near the heads of the Saints, Della Porta left off work. So much of the color was rubbed off, that Mündler could make out in places the outlines of the drawing on the canvas. Attributed to Raphael, with the exception of Morelli and Frizzoni. Most critics date it 1499 or immediately after, considering the work an *ex voto* for the plague that had ravaged Città di Castello in 1499. Cavalcaselle, however, stressed that it was painted after the *Mond Crucifixion* and this opinion was partly accepted by Ortolani, who dated it 1501–4; this period was narrowed down to 1503–4 by Pittaluga, whose opinion was later confirmed by Longhi (1955). The canvas was recently restored to remove the repaints, darkened varnishes, and glues under which the original surface revealed enamels and glazes (S. Liberti, in *Bollettino dell'istituto centrale del restauro*, 1952).

Plate 9B

THE CREATION OF EVE. *Canvas, 166 × 94. Città di Castello, Pinacoteca Comunale*. The reverse, also badly damaged, of the *Standard* for the Church of the Trinity. (See comment on plate 9A.)

Plate 10

THE MOND CRUCIFIXION. *Panel, 279 × 166. London, National Gallery*. The two angels have respectively green and yellow robes. Mary Magdalen, with a pink cloak thrown over a gray-blue robe, stands beside St Jerome, dressed in gray. The Madonna, her gray cloak over a crimson robe, stands near St John whose green robe is cloaked in crimson. At the bottom of the Cross, in golden letters, the inscription runs: RAPHAEL VRBINAS P. The panel was painted for the Gavari Chapel in the Church of San Domenico in Città di Castello, where it was seen by Vasari and described by Lazzari (*Serie dei vescovi di Città di Castello*, Foligno, 1693). At a previous but unknown date it was sold to a Frenchman for 4,000 *scudi*; in 1818 it was in the Fesch Collection, where it was bought for 10,000 *scudi* by

Prince Canino (1845). After passing through various British collections it reached the Mond Collection, and was bequeathed (in 1924) to the National Gallery. Unanimously considered as belonging to the period of Perugino's influence, the work is generally dated 1503 with some tendencies to assign the beginning of the work to 1502. It is worth mentioning, however, that Margherini Graziani (see Biographical Notes) read the date 1503 inscribed on the altar for which it was painted. The predella that formed part of it is divided between Lisbon and the Mrs Derek Fitzgerald Collection (see plates 14 and 15).

Plate 11

THE MOND CRUCIFIXION. Detail showing Christ.

Plate 12

THE MOND CRUCIFIXION. Detail showing Mary Magdalen and St Jerome.

Plate 13

THE MOND CRUCIFIXION. Detail showing the Madonna and St John.

Plate 14

A MIRACLE OF ST CYRIL. *Panel, 23 × 41. Lisbon, Museu Nacional de Arte Antiga*. Panel of the predella which originally formed part of the *Mond Crucifixion*. St Cyril, assisted by St Jerome, revives three dead men. In 1845 Passavant saw it in Rome, attributing it to the School of Perugino. Cavalcaselle already thought the panel a work by the young Raphael, but its connection with the lost Gavari altarpiece is due to Gronau (*Monatshefte für Kunstwissenschaft*, 1908), whose opinion is generally followed by modern critics. Berenson points out some contribution by assistants. There are visible traces of careful restorations in the work.

Plate 15

THE MIRACLE OF ST JEROME. *Panel, 23 × 41. Sussex, Mrs Derek Fitzgerald Collection.* Part of the predella of the *Mond Crucifixion* (see comment on plate 14). The reproduction shows the executioner on the point of beheading Bishop Silvanus: although Jerome holds back his arm, yet miraculously, the heretic is decapitated. The relation with the London painting was established by Gronau (see above).

Plate 16

CORONATION OF THE VIRGIN. *Canvas, 267 × 163; with predella (three scenes transferred to a single canvas), 27 × 187. Rome, Pinacoteca Vaticana.* Commissioned in 1502–3 by Maddalena degli Oddi for her own chapel in the Church of San Francesco in Perugia, where it remained until April 1797, when it was requisitioned by the French who valued it at 1,200 *scudi.* The damage, which shortly before caused the work to be largely restored, induced the Parisian curators to transfer the painting from the original panel to canvas. In 1815 it was returned to Italy and since then has been in the Vatican Art Gallery. The work has been subjected to cleanings and restorations which have left visible traces on the bodies and the landscape. Some old copies are to be found at Civitella Bernazzone in Perugia.

The three sections of the predella, each 27 × 50 (plates 17A, B, and C) are divided by decorative bands, each depicting four small pillars and vegetable motifs on a black background. The sections reproduce the following subjects: the *Annunciation, Epiphany,* and *Presentation in the Temple.* This work has the same history as the *Coronation.* Some damage is noticeable, particularly in the second section. There are partial and faithful copies in museums in Copenhagen, Perugia, and elsewhere.

The whole work is dated by modern critics as 1502 (A. Venturi), 1502–3 (Fischel, Ragghianti, Ortolani, Pittaluga), or 1503 (Berenson, Gamba, Suida, Carli): 1503 seems the most convincing date for the completed work. The work passed through numerous collections. It was originally in the Borghese Palace at Rome, and before reaching its present location, formed part of the Cook Collection at Richmond.

Color Plate I

THE MOND CRUCIFIXION. Detail of plate 10, showing Christ and two angels.

Plate 17A

ANNUNCIATION. Panel of the *Coronation of the Virgin.* See comment on plate 16.

Plate 17B

EPIPHANY. Panel of the *Coronation of the Virgin.* See comment on plate 16.

Plate 17C

PRESENTATION IN THE TEMPLE. Panel of the *Coronation of the Virgin.* See comment on plate 16.

Plate 18

CORONATION OF THE VIRGIN. Detail of the angels, group at left.

Plate 19

CORONATION OF THE VIRGIN. Detail of the angels, group at right.

Plate 20

PORTRAIT OF A MAN. *Panel, 45 × 31. Rome, Borghese Gallery.* An early retouching altered the hat and the clothes; a fur-coat was superimposed under which an embroidered shirt was glimpsed at the neck of the tunic. These additions were brilliantly removed by Cavenaghi in 1911 (E. Modigliani, *L'arte*, 1912). In an inventory dated 1765 (*Inventario di villa Piniciana. . .* , in the archives of the Borghese family), the panel is already listed as a work by Raphael. Later inventories, from the *Fidecommesso artistico nella famiglia Borghese* of 1833 (ibid.) onwards, list it as the work of Holbein. Mündler (*Cicerone*, by Burckhardt, 1869) corrected the attribution, believing it a self-portrait by Perugino, and eventually Morelli (*Zeitschrift für bildende Kunst*, 1874) assigned it to Raphael as a likely portrait of Pinturicchio. After restoration, the Raphael authorship was confirmed by Frizzoni (*Rassegna d'arte*, 1912) and by Ricci (*Pinturicchio*, Perugia, 1915), and maintained by Longhi (*Precisioni. . .* , Rome, 1928). The attribution to Raphael is accepted by the majority of critics with the date 1502 or 1502–3, or perhaps even later, 1503–4. Only A. Venturi continued to accept it as Perugino's self-portrait, dating it 1483–91. Some thought they recognized in this portrait the features of Serafino Aquilano, and Fischel thinks it may be a portrait of Francesco Maria della Rovere (see comment on plate 36).

Plate 21

PORTRAIT OF A GENTLEMAN. *Panel, 55 × 45. Vaduz (Liechtenstein), Collection of the Prince.* The cap is dark and the tones cold; the green jerkin worn under a red coat with a mauve lining and a brown cloak with red lapels. On the back of the painting the following inscription describes its origin: "Gallery of the Marchese Bovio in Bologna in Santo Stefano street. Portrait of a Duke of Urbino in the first manner by Raf.o Sanzio

Urbino." The traditional attribution to Raphael was first denied by Cavalcaselle (*History of North Italian Painting*, I), who thought it by Francia, but Cavalcaselle later accepted the attribution (1884), although with some hesitation and at the same time stressing the influence of Francia. A. Venturi did not think it was a portrait of the Duke of Urbino nor did he ascribe the work to Raphael (*Storia. . .* , Milan, 1914, VII, 3); he attributed it to Meloni. This theory found some support, although when in Vienna the painting was listed as by Francia. Filippini (*Cronache d'arte*, September–October 1925) reverted to the old Raphaelesque attribution, placing it in the period of Raphael's activity in Bologna which occurred, according to him, in 1506. Filippini thinks the panel a portrait of Guidobaldo d'Urbino, and this is apparently confirmed by its resemblance to the portrait in the Uffizi and by the dark cloak of the Order of the Garter. The link with Bembo's letter to Bibbiena in 1516 and with the news given by Baldi therefore appears valid (see comment on plate 92). Filippini, however, also suggests that the portrait might be by Francia based on a drawing by Raphael. It was attributed to Raphael by Berenson and Longhi (1955), and Longhi dates it 1503–4. Gronau considers it to be a copy and a portrait of Guidobaldo, though this last hypothesis is denied by critics nowadays. The central part of the painting, in the region of the lower part of the face, has lost its coating.

Plate 22

THE MARRIAGE OF THE VIRGIN. *Panel, 170 × 117. Milan, Brera Gallery.* On the cornice of the temple the signature: RAPHAEL VRBINAS; on the spandrels below, the date: MDIIII. Surrounding the priest in front of the church—which has been connected with the building erected by Bramante in the courtyard of San Pietro in Montorio (1502) and with the Temple of Neptune in Rome —are: Mary, followed by five friends, and Joseph with an equal number of disappointed suitors behind him; in the last but one suitor to the right, some recognize the features of Raphael himself. The panel was commissioned by the Albizzini family for the Chapel of St Joseph in the Church of San Francesco in Città di Castello, where it was seen by Vasari and Pungileoni. In 1798 it was given by the municipal authorities to the Napoleonic General, Lechi, who sold it (1801) to a businessman, Sannazzari, for 50,000 *liras*. Sannazzari (1804) bequeathed it to the Maggiore Ospedale in Milan. In 1806 it was bought by the Beauharnais government for the Milan Academy. Towards the end of the nineteenth century, it was restored by Molteni, and to him, together with some predecessors, a cleaning is due which in some places has taken away the surface area. A copy of the painting by a certain Urbini is reported at Urbino, with the inscription: RAPHAEL INVENTOR.

Plate 23

THE MARRIAGE OF THE VIRGIN. Detail showing central group.

Plate 24

THE MARRIAGE OF THE VIRGIN. Bust of the Virgin.

Plate 25

THE MARRIAGE OF THE VIRGIN. Detail showing the suitor breaking his staff.

Plate 26

THE MARRIAGE OF THE VIRGIN. The heads of Mary's bridesmaids.

Plate 27

THE MARRIAGE OF THE VIRGIN. Heads of suitors.

Plate 28

THE DIOTALLEVI MADONNA. *Panel, 69 × 50. Berlin, Staatliche Museen.* Was bought by the Kaiser Friedrich Museum in 1841-2 for 980 *thalers* from the Marchese Diotallevi of Rimini, in whose family the painting had long been, as a work by Perugino. The panel is almost unanimously attributed to Raphael, but variously dated 1500 (Fischel), 1501 (Ortolani), or 1502 (Rosenberg). Cavalcaselle links it with the *Consolation Madonna* (Perugia), completed by Perugino in 1498 but started in 1496. It is, however, likely that Raphael was inspired by this Madonna some years later, perhaps in 1502 or 1503, and only completed the work in 1504 (Longhi, 1955). A. Venturi (*Storia...*, Milan, 1913, VII, 2) attributed it to the unknown "Master of the Diotallevi Madonna" who is supposed to have worked with Perugino on the *Consolation Madonna*. Abrasions, fading of colors, cleanings, and restorations markedly reduce the quality of this painting.

Plate 29

PORTRAIT OF A YOUNG MAN. *Panel, 54 × 39. Budapest, Museum of Fine Arts.* The sitter, with red cap and dress and deep violet cloak, was recognized by Passavant as being Francesco Maria della Rovere, but this identification was not generally accepted. Fischel calls it *Young Secretary*, stressing that the subject's clothing is that of a Humanist. The panel came to Budapest in 1820 from the Esterhazy Collection and was attributed to Luini. Viardot was the first critic to be convinced of Raphael's authorship (*Les Museés de l'Allemagne et de Russie*, Paris, 1844), and was followed by Passavant, Morelli (1886), Frimmel (*Galerie-studien*, Bamberg, 1892), Pulzky (*Archaelogia Értesitö*, 1896) dating it 1505–6 and, in modern times, by Berenson, Gronau, Burkhalter (*Die Bildnisse Rafaels*, Berne, 1932), Ortolani, Fischel, Suida, who generally date it 1504. These critics believe the work to be entirely authentic with the exception of Berenson, who notices some few contributions by assistants. Other critics consider it the work of a Florentine; Cust (*The Burlington Magazine*, 1916) tentatively suggests Ridolfo del Ghirlandaio. The painting has been subjected to extensive restorations.

Plate 30

THE TERRANUOVA MADONNA. *Circular panel, diameter 87. Berlin, Staatliche Museen.* The holy child on the right has not been identified. It is not known how this painting was acquired by the Dukes of Terranuova, in whose possession it long remained, first at Genoa then at Naples, where it was acquired in 1854 for its present home for 30,000 *scudi*. The panel is almost unanimously dated 1505 although it was more probably executed earlier, in 1504, as maintained by Gamba, and Longhi more precisely, in the last months of that year. There is some slight damage in the center band, particularly in the figures of John the Baptist and Christ.

Plate 31

THE CONNESTABILE MADONNA. *Circular canvas, diameter 17·9. Leningrad, Hermitage.* Originally painted on wood. When transferred to canvas towards the end of the last century it was discovered that the original drawing was a faithful reproduction of the Berlin cartoon in which Jesus is playing with an apple held by Mary. The Madonna's red robe is cloaked in blue; the cover of the book is dark brown; in the right background a snow-covered mountain—a rare sight in Italian pictures. According to some published memoirs by A. Rossi (*Giornale d'erudizione artistica*, VI), the work seems to have belonged to Alfano di Diamante, uncle of Domenico di Paris Alfani, a friend of Raphael, and to have been handed down through the collateral branch of the Connestabile Staffa. It was certainly sold, on April 21, 1871, by Count Scipione Connestabile of Perugia to the Russian Empress for 330,000 francs and so came to its present home. The panel is unanimously attributed to Raphael. Gronau, Gamba, Fischel, and A. Venturi, date it 1500–2; Ortolani and Carli, date it, with some doubts 1504; in 1955 Longhi has clearly explained why the work was executed at the end of that year, since the painting already belongs to the Florentine period.

Plate 32

SELF-PORTRAIT. *Panel, 52 × 41. Munich, Alte Pinakothek.* The sitter, wearing a black cap, is shown between two columns of mottled marble against a landscape which Volpe (*Paragone*, 1956) rightly relates to that of the *Baptist* painted by Memling (a work then probably in Italy in the Bembo Collection and now also in the Munich Pinakothek).

The doublet with sleeves of pomegranate red and the silk cloak over it are rather dark. On the golden buttons of the doublet Gruyer reads; RAPHAELLO VRBINAS FEC. and so did later students, while Volpe himself reads RAFFAELLO URBINATE, an inscription which seems scientifically proved. Up to the eighteenth century this work belonged to the Del Riccio family in Florence, where it was acquired by J. Hugford as a work by Raphael. Mengs certified it on January 17, 1774 with a document attached to the reverse of the painting: "The undersigned has seen and studied the above-mentioned painting and judges it to be by the hand of Raphael of Urbino." After being in the collection of Count Firmian at Leopoldskron, it passed to Ludwig I, King of Bavaria, and then to its present home. Passavant maintains Raphael's authorship, shortly afterwards denied by Gruyer, who presumed the signature false and stressed the panel's likeness with the *Portrait of a Young Man* at Hampton Court. Cavalcaselle was equally in favor of a different painter, perhaps Alfani, and thought the inscription was a later addition. Morelli agreed, stressing the Umbrian character of the painting. Gruyer's opinions are reflected in the catalogues of the Alte Pinakothek from 1885 onwards, where the work is ascribed to an unknown "Umbrian-Bolognese master, *circa* 1510." This attribution remained unchanged until 1936 when, in the catalogue compiled by Buchner, it is altered to "School of Ferrara-Bologna, *circa* 1510." Berenson (*Italian Paintings of the Renaissance*, Oxford, 1932) dubiously suggested the name of Aspertini. In the most recent catalogue of the Munich Gallery (1953) we find the panel described as "Bolognese-Umbrian, *circa* 1505" and the sitter identified as "the young Raphael." This identification has been confirmed by Volpe on the basis of a comparison with the self-portrait in the *School of Athens* at the Vatican. Volpe also reverts to the early attribution to Raphael, dating the painting 1504-5 because of Florentine characteristics. The work is badly preserved, having lost the coating on part of the hair, face, neck, and hand, and also because of incompetent repainting.

Color Plate II

VISION OF A KNIGHT. Detail of plate 44, showing landscape in background.

Plate 33

THE VEILED WOMAN. *Panel, 74 × 50. Hanover, Landesgalerie*. This painting passed to the Kestner Collection in the first half of the nineteenth century from Bologna, and from there to its present location. The work was traditionally attributed to Raphael, but Passavant was the first to consider this doubtful. Cavalcaselle favored a follower of Sebastiano del Piombo. Rosenberg and Gronau excluded it from the body of Raphael's works. Küppers (*Monatsheft für Kunstwissenschaft*, 1916) attributed it to Sebastiano del Piombo as did Gombosi (*Allgemeines Lexikon*, Thieme-Becker-Vollmer, eds., Leipzig, 1933, XXXVI); Dussler (*Sebastiano del Piombo*, Basel, 1942) and Pallucchini (*Sebastian Viniziano*, Milan, 1944) vehemently disagreed. Although A. Venturi and Berenson (the latter dubiously) suggested Pippi, Fischel remained in favor of Raphael and his opinion found support in such scholars as Putscher, who compiled the catalogue of the Landesgalerie (Hanover, 1954), Longhi (1955), and Volpe (*Paragone*, 1956). Longhi dates the work around 1504, instead of the

43

usually proposed Roman period. It was restored several times between 1892 and 1950, and further restorations are needed.

Plate 34

PORTRAIT OF ELISABETTA GON-ZAGA. *Panel, 58 × 36. Florence, Uffizi.* On the reverse is the inscription: "Isabella Mantovana, wife of the Duke Guido." This does not contradict identification with Elisabetta, wife of Guidobaldo di Montefeltro, as "Isabella" is possibly a distortion of "Isabetta", which was how she normally signed her name. The panel is already mentioned as being a portrait of the Duchess of Urbino by Morelli and, a little later, by Luzio and Renier (*Mantova e Urbino,* 1893), but the decisive identification is due to Delaruelle (*L'arte,* 1900). The painting remained in the collections of the Dukes of Urbino up to 1631, when it was transferred to the Medici and was exhibited in the Uffizi *tribuna* as a work by Mantegna. Burckhardt (*Der Cicerone,* Basel, 1855) could not choose between Caroto and Bonsignori; it was attributed to the latter by Cavalcaselle (*Storia. . . ,* Florence, 1886); Morelli, though with doubts, favored Caroto and was supported by Berenson. The first reference to Raphael was made by Durand-Gréville (*Revue de l'art ancien et moderne,* 1905) but this received no support and was dismissed by Gronau (*Repertorium für Kunstwissenschaft,* 1907); later, however, Gronau confirmed the attribution (*Bollettino d'arte,* 1925), and this was rapidly accepted by Berenson and others (Ortolani, Longhi, etc.). Salvini, too (*Galleria degli Uffizi,* Florence, 1952), seems in favor of Raphael, but without abandoning the opinion of A. Venturi (*Storia. . . ,* Milan, 1914, VII, 3) that the portrait was probably

related to Francia's School. The indications of Francia led Ortolani to put forward the hypothesis that it might be a work begun by Giovanni Santi and completed by Raphael, his son. If this is so, because of elements that indicate the Florentine period, one should assume that the work was painted at two quite different periods: and so, while Gronau dates it 1505–6, Ortolani favors 1504, a date which is possible if one takes it to mean the last month of that year. The attribution to Tamaroccio made by Filippini (*Cronache d'arte,* 1955), who maintained the sitter was Elisabetta (A. Venturi doubts this) has not been supported.

Plate 35

EMILIA PIA OF MONTEFELTRO. *Panel, 42·5 × 28·5. Baltimore, Epstein Collection.* On the reverse, in sixteenth–seventeenth century characters is the inscription: "Emilia Pia da Montefeltro." The identification of the sitter as being the friend and executor of Elisabetta Gonzaga (Dennistoun, *Memoirs of the Dukes of Urbino,* London, 1909) is proved by its likeness to the portrait on a medal attributed by Fabriczy to Adriano Fiorentino (*Jahrbuch der preussischen Kunstsammlungen,* 1903). The painting may have been in the collections of the Dukes of Urbino and it is probably listed, in an inventory (1654) of the artistic patrimony of the Della Rovere—the inventory later passed to the Medici family. The work's transfer to Vienna might explain the seal on the back with the inscription which may, perhaps, have read: "[Fo]ntico tedesco di V[enezia]." In the Austrian capital the panel was cleaned by Sikora before it was acquired for the Covay-Stoop Collection in Erlenbach

(Zürich) in 1925. It then passed to the E. Kleinberger Gallery (New York) and thence to its present location. The attribution to Raphael proposed by Gronau (*Bolletino d'arte*, 1925) was accepted by Berenson and Longhi (1955) and others. The work is datable at the end of 1504 because of its affinities with the previous painting (see comment on plate 34). The panel is, except for some old cracks, well preserved.

Plate 36

YOUNG MAN WITH AN APPLE. *Panel, 47 × 35. Florence, Uffizi.* In 1631 this painting was transferred from the collection of the Dukes of Urbino to the Medici family as part of the bequest of Vittoria della Rovere, and was hung in the Pitti Palace, where it remained until recently. It is believed to be by a pupil of Francia (A. Venturi, *Storia . . . ,* Milan, 1914, VII, 3) or by Francia's son, Giacomo (Durand-Gréville, *Revue de l'art ancien et moderne*, 1905). Durand-Gréville identified the sitter as Francesco Maria della Rovere. The panel was thought to be by Raphael and the attribution was accepted by Gronau (1909), Gamba, and Longhi (1955), while Fischel, M. Marangoni, Ortolani, Salvini (*Galleria degli Uffizi*, Florence, 1952, *et seq.*), Suida, etc., accepted the attribution with doubts (see comment on plate 149). The work is variously dated between 1503 and 1505, half-way between the two dates seeming most probable. The attribution to Tamaroccio made by Filippini (*Cronache d'Arte*, 1925) was not accepted.

Plate 37

THE COLONNA ALTARPIECE, *Central panel, 68 × 68; lunette, 30 × 68. New York, Metropolitan Museum of Art.* In the center panel of the painting, on either side of the enthroned Madonna with her Child on her knees leaning towards the small St John, are the Saints Peter and Catherine to the left and Paul and Cecilia (or Margaret) on the right. The altarpiece was commissioned by the nuns of St Anthony in Perugia. Vasari writes that the Christ Child appears dressed "in a manner pleasing to those simple and venerable women." The oldest record relates to the sale of the painting: in 1677 the nuns, who were the owners, asked for permission to sell it. On May 8 of the same year the central panel and lunette were bought by a nobleman of Perugia, Antonio Bigazzini, for 2,000 *scudi*. Sold to the Colonna Princes of Rome, it was later acquired for the collection of Francis I, King of the Two Sicilies; Francis II took it with him from Gaeta to Spain (1861); after having passed through several hands it was bought (1901) by Pierpoint Morgan for 50,000 dollars, who bequeathed it (1916) to the Metropolitan Museum. The work was dated around 1504 by Fischel and Suida, 1504–5 by Ortolani, and 1505 by Berenson and Carli. Cavalcaselle had already pointed out that it was executed at two quite distinct periods; the beginning during the Perugia period and the completion during the artist's return to Umbria after he had moved to Florence in 1504. This opinion was accepted by Gronau (who suggests the date 1503–5) and by L. Venturi (*Pitture italiane in America*, Milan, 1931), and confirmed by Longhi (1955). Paliard (*Gazette des Beaux-Arts*, 1877) maintained that the group comprising Mary with Christ and John the Baptist was copied from a painting by Bernardino di Mariotto in the Perugia Gallery, but Cavalcaselle proved the contrary.

Originally the predella was sold together with its predella by the nuns of St Anthony (1663) to Christina of Sweden for 600 *scudi*. After passing through other collections the predella alone was auctioned in 1798 at the sale of the Orléans Collection. Some panels are in London (plates 40–41c), the Metropolitan Museum in New York (plates 40–41A), in Boston (plates 40–41B), and in Dulwich (plates 39A and B). A. Venturi thought he had identified another panel of the predella in the Gemäldegalerie, Dresden (see page 115). A copy of the predella executed by Inglesio Gallo in 1663 for the Church of St Anthony in Perugia depicts the original position of the three main panels.

Plate 38

THE COLONNA ALTARPIECE. Detail of the central panel showing the Madonna and the infant Christ and John.

Plate 39A

A FRANCISCAN SAINT. *Panel, 24 × 16. Dulwich, College Gallery*. Usually described as a small pillar—probably on the extreme left—of the dismantled predella of the *Colonna Altarpiece* (see comment on plate 37). It is possible, however, that originally in the whole altarpiece it occupied a different place, if we are to take into account the dimensions of the various other panels believed to have been parts of the same predella. The panel is badly preserved (the lower part of the face is repainted); its dimensions have been altered because of the addition to the right side of the panel of a piece which occupies the whole height and is almost two inches wide. In general, the critics, though relating it to the whole work executed in 1505

for the nuns of St Anthony in Perugia, are reluctant to consider this panel a work by Raphael. Nevertheless, Berenson's opinion that not only the concept but also part of the execution is Raphael's seems acceptable.

Plate 39B

ST ANTHONY OF PADUA. *Panel, 24 × 16. Dulwich, College Gallery*. The twin of the previous painting (see comment on plate 38A). It reveals similar characteristics and damage (the repainting on the face is more widespread, and the addition has been made on the left side). In the predella of the *Colonna Altarpiece*, or at least near it, this panel must have been on the right side.

Plate 40–41A

THE AGONY IN THE GARDEN. *Panel, 24 × 28. New York, Metropolitan Museum of Art*. Panel of the dismantled predella of the *Colonna Altarpiece* (see comment on plate 37); it formed part of the left side of it. From the Orléans Collection it passed through successive English collections, and was recently acquired by the Metropolitan Museum. Cavalcaselle, among others, attributed only the concept of the panel to Raphael, considering it was executed by an assistant. Modern critics tend to believe it largely an authentic work by Raphael. It shows traces of major repainting in the upper part, in the center, and on the right, down as far as about Christ's waist.

Plate 40–41B

PIETÀ. *Panel, 24 × 28. Boston, Isabella Stewart Gardner Museum*. Panel of the *Colonna Altarpiece* predella, on the right of the *Ascent to Calvary*. Sold for £60 at the auction of the Orléans Collection, the panel went successively through various European collections, reaching its present location in 1909. The work is unanimously believed to be by Raphael and dated 1505, although not all critics agree in relating it to the *Colonna Altarpiece*. If the descriptions of early critics are to be believed, the panel must recently have been subjected to vigorous cleaning in the course of which, among other things, even the nails which Cavalcaselle remembers in the hands of Nicodemus have disappeared.

Plate 40–41C

ASCENT TO CALVARY. *Panel, 23 × 85. London, National Gallery.* Central panel of the predella. From the Orléans Collection it went for £150 to Mr W. Miles of Leigh Court; in 1884 it went for £560 to the collection of Lord Windsor; in 1913 it was acquired by the National Gallery. Cavalcaselle tended to date the work after August 1505, seeing in the group of the Marys a derivation from a similar group painted by Perugino in the Florentine *Deposition*, later left unfinished by Lippi (see page 115). Longhi (1955) seems to favor a date after the *Ansidei Altarpiece*, suggesting 1506. Several critics notice in it important (Cavalcaselle) or slight (Berenson) contributions by assistants.

Plate 42

THE GRANDUCA MADONNA. *Panel, 84 × 55. Florence, Pitti Palace.* Acquired in 1799 for 300 *sequins* by Ferdinand III of Hapsburg-Lorraine, this painting owes its name to the fact that the Grand Duke was so attached to it that it accompanied him on all his travels. It had pre-viously belonged to Carlo Dolci. The work is almost unanimously dated 1505, during Raphael's Florentine period and a little before the frescos in San Severo at Perugia. Suida suggests a slightly earlier date, 1504–5, which, according to Longhi (1955) should be even earlier, coinciding with the arrival of Raphael in Florence (1504). Repainting is noticeable on the bodies, and Mary's blue cloak is disfigured by blotches. Above all, it would seem that the background was painted at a much later date, so that the true date of the work may differ again from the above suggestions. In this case, one should date it about 1506 or, definitely, 1507.

Plate 43

THE SMALL COWPER MADONNA. *Panel, 58 × 43. Washington, National Gallery of Art.* After remaining in a private collection in Urbino until 1780, this painting was bought by the third Lord Cowper of Panshanger (from whom it derives its name, while the adjective is used to distinguish it from another Madonna, also in Washington, once also in Lord Cowper's possession). In 1913 it was acquired by Duveen; in 1917 by Joseph Widener (Philadelphia), from whom it recently passed to its present location. Gamba dates it at the end of 1506 "since the Church of San Bernardino in Urbino is depicted in the background, one presumes that it was painted there." The dating of about 1505 by Fischel, L. Venturi (*Pitture italiane in America*, Milan, 1931), and Suida seems more accurate. Longhi suggests 1504–5. Cavalcaselle noted some contribution by assistants, but this might also be inexpert restoration. There is mention of a copy, perhaps contemporary with the original, which is probably the one seen by Passavant in the home of the Peruzzi family in Florence and which later passed to the Lombardi Collection in the same city.

Plate 44

VISION OF A KNIGHT. *Panel, 17 × 17. London, National Gallery.* The subject was variously interpreted as *Hercules at the Cross-roads*, *Hercules among the Hesperides*, and *The Dream of Scipio*. For a long time it was kept in the Borghese Collection in Rome, and towards the end of the eighteenth century it passed to W. Y. Ottley; it was successively in several English collections before its acquisition by the National Gallery. The critics are unanimous in attributing it to Raphael; but, contrary to Cavalcaselle, who dated it 1504 (that is, immediately before his Florentine stay), later scholars dated the work earlier, 1500 or even 1498–1500, considering it as one of the artist's very first works. Suida, however, dates it 1500–2, but even this does not explain the already perfect "classicism" emphasized by Longhi (1955) who dates it 1504–5. The source, the probable affinity of subject, the chronological nearness, and even the dimensions led Panofsky to conclude that this painting was once part of the *Three Graces* in Chantilly (plate 45), with which it formed a small diptych.

Plate 45

THE THREE GRACES. *Panel, 17 × 17. Chantilly, Musée Condé.* The title of this painting is traditional. Cavalcaselle saw in it a derivation from the classical group given by Pius II to the Piccolomini Library of Siena; the presence of the apples suggested the possibility that the figures represented the Hesperides. Suida linked it to the back of a

medal by Niccolò di Forzore Spinelli which portrayed Giovanna degli Albizzi, who married Lorenzo Tornabuoni in 1486. He reasoned that while, in the old Sienese group, the three figures are armless, the three maidens on the medal correspond "perfectly" to those painted by Raphael; the medal itself bears the inscription "*Castitas, Pulchritudo, Amor.*" The painting was in the Borghese Collection in Rome from as early as 1650 (Manili, *Villa Borghese*, Rome, 1650); after about 1800 it belonged successively to several English collections and was acquired by the Musée Condé in 1885. Most critics date it around 1500; Pittaluga dates it 1498–1500, Gamba 1499, Gronau and Fischel about 1500, A. Venturi 1501, Ortolani 1501–2, Suida about 1502. Carli, stressing the stylistic maturity of the work, dated it, though doubtfully, 1504; Longhi (1955) attributes it to Raphael's first Florentine period, i.e. 1504–5. In an excellent state of preservation, the panel has perhaps suffered slight loss of patina. For its relation to the *Vision of a Knight*, see the comment on plate 44.

Plate 46

ST MICHAEL AND THE DEMON. *Panel, 31 × 27. Paris, The Louvre.* The Archangel wears a blue robe and golden armor; his wings are green and the cross on the shield is red. Cavalcaselle compares its "Dantesque" landscape and the monsters with the *Temptation of St Anthony* by Jerome Bosch which was perhaps known to Raphael through an engraving. Müntz, on the basis of information advanced by Lomazzo, believes that it was commissioned with the *St George* in the Louvre, by Guidobaldo d'Urbino; this theory, however, was dismissed by Cavalcaselle. It is certain that, together with the *St George*, it belonged in the seventeenth century to Cardinal Mazarin (who possibly bought both paintings when Charles I of England's Collection was dispersed) and that his heirs sold both works to Louis XIV. In this way they passed to the Louvre. It is therefore probably necessary to take into account the most necessary theories about it.

Fischel dates it 1500, A. Venturi 1501, Gronau 1500–2, and Suida about 1502; Gamba dates it around 1504, a date which is accepted by Rosenberg and narrowed down to the last months of that year by Ortolani, Carli, and others; but perhaps it would be more correct to date it later, i.e. 1505. Gamba and others believed that this painting originally formed a diptych with the already mentioned *St George* and the identical dimensions, the stylistic affinity, the analogy of composition, and the common history they share may prove this theory correct. One should remember, however, not only the difference in chronology maintained by several critics, but also the lack of symmetry in the two works.

Plate 47

ST MICHAEL AND THE DEMON. Detail of the background at left.

Plate 48

ST GEORGE AND THE DRAGON. *Panel, 31 × 27. Paris, The Louvre.* The Saint is clad in golden armor; the horse is gray, the spear red and white; the Princess's robe is pinkish. The panel shares the history of *St Michael and the Demon* and is similarly dated (see comment on plate 46), even by Ortolani who, however, insists that the *St George* was painted after the *St Michael*. Pittaluga favors the date 1504–5, but

the panel should perhaps be dated 1505. One should note that in a recent essay by Lynch (*Gazette des Beaux-Arts*, April 1962), this work is identified as the one sent in 1506 to the King of England by Guidobaldo di Montefeltro, which was hitherto identified with the same subject in Washington (plate 62). Lynch's theory is not without foundation; should it be proved, it will be necessary to re-examine the chronology of the paintings.

Color Plate III

THE ANSIDEI ALTARPIECE. Detail showing Madonna and Child.

Plate 49

THE ANSIDEI ALTARPIECE. *Panel, 274 × 152. London, National Gallery.* The enthroned Madonna and Child are depicted reading between John the Baptist and St Nicholas of Bari dressed in the robes of his office with three golden spheres, the emblem of his sanctity, at his feet. Above the Virgin's throne is the inscription: SALVE.MATER.CHRISTI. Painted in Perugia for the Ansidei family (Vasari), it was erected in 1506 in the family chapel in the Church of San Fiorenzo dei Serviti, where Lord R. Spenser bought it in 1764, promising to substitute for it a copy painted by Nicola Monti. This is still there. The original passed to the Duke of Marlborough, from whose collection it was acquired by the National Gallery (1885) for the sum of £70,000. On the edge of Mary's cloak beneath her left hand a date was noted by Passavant and Waagen (*Art Treasures in Great Britain*, London, 1854) as being MDV, but Cavalcaselle read it correctly as MDVI. Other critics, however, have read it as MDVII. Such differences have a bearing on the date of the work, thought by some to be 1505, but most critics date it as late as 1505–6 or 1506; Pittaluga thinks the date was 1504–5. Cavalcaselle rightly assumed that Raphael executed this work during two different periods, beginning it before his stay in Florence (1504) and finishing it on his return to Umbria (1506); this theory is confirmed by Longhi (1955), who believes the work was conceived before the altarpiece for the Church of St Anthony of Perugia, and accepts 1506 as the date of completion. The altarpiece seems well preserved, except for traces of cleaning along the edges. Of the original predella only one panel is known, in the Viscountess Mersey Collection (plate 53); the two others, depicting the *Marriage of the Virgin* and a *Miracle of St Nicholas of Bari*, remained in Italy when the altarpiece was taken apart and are in different locations.

Plate 50

THE ANSIDEI ALTARPIECE. Detail of John the Baptist.

Plate 51

THE ANSIDEI ALTARPIECE. Detail of the Madonna.

Plate 52

THE ANSIDEI ALTARPIECE. Detail of St Nicholas of Bari.

Plate 53

JOHN THE BAPTIST PREACHING. *Panel, 26 × 53.3. Sussex, Viscountess Mersey Collection.* The only known panel of the *Ansidei Altarpiece* (see comment on plate 49), whose history it shared up to the time the altarpiece was acquired by Lord Spenser. Later, from the Philipp auction (1828), it was acquired for the Lansdowne Collection. For the dates of execution, the reader should refer to what has

been said about the *Ansidei Altarpiece*, with which this panel was conceived and executed during two periods: about 1504 and 1506. The other two panels of the predella depict the *Marriage of the Virgin* and a *Miracle of St Nicholas of Bari*. One should assume that originally each of these panels was meant to be placed under the appropriate character portrayed in the *Altarpiece*.

Plate 54

THE NORTHBROOK MADONNA. *Panel, 66 × 37. London, Lord Northbrook Collection.* This painting, which came from the American collection of T. H. J. Ellis, is already listed in the privately printed catalogue of the Northbrook Collection in 1889. The attribution to Raphael proposed by A. Venturi was accepted by Ortolani and Longhi (1955), refuted by Gronau (who referred to Cavalcaselle's mention of Spagna), and ignored by several scholars. A. Venturi links it with the *St George* in the Louvre; Ortolani suggests a later date, towards 1508; Longhi (1955) dates the work 1505–6 because of its affinity to the *Connestabile Madonna* on the one hand, and the *Esterhazy Madonna* on the other.

Plate 55

THE ESTERHAZY MADONNA. *Panel, 29 × 21.5. Budapest, Museum of Fine Arts.* On the scroll held by the Baptist are the words ECCE AGNUS DEI. The ruins in the left background reminded Cavalcaselle of the Temple of Vespasian in Rome. On the reverse of the panel a slip of paper is pasted containing a reference to the gift made by Pope Clement XI to Empress Elizabeth; the latter apparently presented this picture to Prince Kaunitz, on whose death it came into the possession of the

Esterhazy family. The panel is unanimously attributed to Raphael. Cavalcaselle, pointing out the differences between the background of the small cartoon at the Uffizi representing a river landscape and that of this painting, thought that this panel was executed during the artist's Roman period. This hypothesis was supported by other critics, including Gronau, Gamba, and Suida, who suggested the date of about 1508, and Rosenberg, who favored 1508–10. Among the critics who opposed the theory are A. Venturi and Fischel (who dates the panel 1505–7), and other more contemporary scholars, including Longhi (1955), who connects the painting with the *Northbrook Madonna*, dating it 1505–6. The condition of the work, considered unfinished by Berenson, makes an accurate decision difficult; one must, however, place it within the first years of the Florentine period—at least from the point of view of its conception.

Plate 56

THE ORLÉANS MADONNA. *Panel, 29 × 21. Chantilly, Musée Condé*. Mary wears a red robe with a dark green sash and a blue cloak with a brown lining; the curtain is dark gray. The panel is generally identified as one of the two small Madonnas noted by Vasari (though with some imprecision) as painted for Guidobaldo di Montefeltro when Raphael returned to his native town in 1507, and seen by Vasari in the home of Guidobaldo, Duke of Urbino. The following particularly noteworthy statement appears in the inventory of the Ducal Palace of Urbino: "Small painting of a Madonna with Jesus in her arms, on wood, by Raphael."

The work was the property of the brother of Louis XIV of France and later passed to the Orléans family. It was acquired successively by various collections before being bought in 1869 by the Duke d'Aumale for 150,000 francs. From his collection it went to its present location. The only doubt as to the absolute authenticity of the work is that of Passavant, who considered the background had been repainted by a follower of Teniers; Cavalcaselle, however, dismissed this theory.

According to information given by Vasari, the panel was usually dated 1507 or immediately after; it is, however, wise to accept the modern tendency to date it 1506, though Fischel favors 1505. The work is excellently preserved.

Plate 57

VIRGIN AND CHILD WITH BEARDLESS ST JOSEPH. *Canvas, 74 × 57. Leningrad, Hermitage*. This painting was mistakenly identified by Passavant as a work listed in an inventory of the ancient collections of the Dukes of Urbino. The work actually listed is a *Holy Family with Palm* (plate 58). The panel should possibly be identified as one of the two paintings noted by Vasari as having been painted by Raphael in Florence for Taddeo Taddei. We have, however, no record of it until the seventeenth century when it apparently belonged to the Duke d'Angoulême in Paris; it was then sold to a certain Barroy; cleaned by Vendine, the panel passed to the Crozat Collection (still in France) and then to its present location. The attribution to Raphael is unanimous. Gamba and Fischel, among others, date it 1505 or thereabouts; Gronau, Ortolani, and others more correctly date it 1506. Poor restoration has obviously injured the faces of all the figures and Christ's legs.

Plate 58

HOLY FAMILY WITH PALM. *Circular panel, diameter 101·4. London, Ellesmere Collection.* According to Cavalcaselle the surroundings recall "a landscape near Lake Trasimeno." Under a light cloak Joseph wears a purple tunic; Mary wears a blue cloak over a red gown with bright sleeves that range from violet tones in the shadow to yellow in the light, with a pink undersleeve. Milanesi tentatively identifies it as one of the two pictures Raphael painted in Florence for Taddeo Taddei and mentioned by Vasari as being in the possession of the latter's heirs who, however, did not own them at the time of Baldinucci (*Notizie. . . ,* Florence, 1681).

This theory appears more credible than that identifying the panel as one of two works (Vasari) completed for Guidobaldo di Montefeltro during Raphael's stay at Urbino in 1507. This hypothesis attempts to link the panel with an entry in the inventory of the Urbino family's Collections. This entry refers more probably to the *Virgin and Child with Beardless St Joseph* in Leningrad. Reliable records go back no further than the seventeenth century: before 1680 the painting belonged to the Countess de Chiverni in Paris; after changing hands several times it became the property of the Duke of Orléans; at the sale of his collection (1792), it was acquired by the Earl of Ellesmere for £1,200. The earlier dates for this panel vary between about 1505 and 1507, but another chronology, dating the work slightly after the completion of the *Orléans Madonna,* seems more accurate. The painting bears traces of restoration carried out especially to cover two vertical splits. The halos have almost disappeared.

Faint traces of letters on the neck of the dress might have been the artist's signature.

Plate 59

CHRIST BLESSING. *Panel, 30 × 25. Brescia, Pinacoteca Tosio Martinengo.* Known also as *Pax Vobis,* this painting comes from the Mosca family of Pesaro, from whom Count Tosio bought it in 1832. The hip-cloth worn by Jesus is colored red. Fischel dates it 1502, Gronau 1502–3, A. Venturi and Ortolani 1503, but Cavalcaselle linked it with the painter's Florentine period, dating it 1504. Gamba correctly dates the beginning of the painting 1506, but extends the period of execution too much, until 1508. Some slight loss of patina is evident on the panel.

Plate 60

SELF-PORTRAIT. *Panel, 45 × 33. Florence, Uffizi.* This work was probably in Urbino until transferred by Federico Zuccari in 1588 to the Academy of San Luca in Rome. The Academy sold the painting shortly after to Cardinal Leopold de' Medici, in whose Will we find it definitely mentioned for the first time (1675). This work is damaged by bad restoration which have dulled the colors and altered the forms; its size also appears to have been reduced on the left side. Critics have always agreed on Raphael's authorship and on the date, about 1506; recently Volpe (*Paragone,* 1956) considered it an enigma "because of the wretched state of preservation which prevents one from establishing its authenticity."

Plate 61

PORTRAIT OF A YOUNG WOMAN. *Panel, 65 × 51. Rome, Borghese Gallery.* This painting, which is also known as *The Lady of the Unicorn,* was repainted by a Florentine artist towards the middle of the sixteenth century, and until 1935 the portrait was said to represent St Catherine. However, the same subject mentioned by Manilli (*Villa Borghese*, Rome, 1650) and by Rossini (1725) is to be identified as the painting now in London (plate 89). The work is listed in the 1760 inventories of the Borghese family as a work by Perugino, to whose style and School it was attributed in the inventory notes, Morelli (*Zeitschrift für bildende Kunst*, 1874) first suggested Ridolfo del Ghirlandaio, then Granacci, or a painter of the same School, who had based this work on Raphael's drawing (in the Louvre) for the *Portrait of Maddalena Doni*.

The panel was also attributed to Granacci by Berenson, and A. Venturi (1893) suggested, though dubiously, the young Andrea del Sarto. Cantalamessa (*Bollettino d'arte*, 1916) noted the work of two different artists, to the second of whom he attributed the execution of the cloak, the hands, and the symbols of martyrdom; these he thought additions to the work of the first painter. In 1925, A. Venturi, changing his mind, attributed it to Ridolfo del Ghirlandaio. Shortly afterwards, however, Longhi (*Vita artistica*, 1927) confirmed Cantalamessa's theory, shedding further light on the extent of the additions. This led to an X-ray examination of the panel which revealed the original appearance of the painting, as it may be seen today, in which the unicorn is a symbol of chastity. Following further contributions by Longhi (*Pinacoteca*, 1928, and *Precisini nelle gallerie italiane*, Rome, 1928), restoration was begun and revealed how the original work had been damaged (the background, the shoulders, and the figure of the unicorn) and why the additions had been made. The

attribution to Raphael already advanced by Longhi was accepted by De Rinaldis (*Bollettino d'arte*, 1936) and eventually by almost all critics, with dates varying between 1505 and 1506. Ortolani is of the opinion that this is the "true" *Maddalena Doni*, but the dimensions and composition are too different from the *Angelo Doni* in Florence (plate 68).

Plate 62

ST GEORGE AND THE DRAGON. *Panel, 28 × 22. Washington, National Gallery of Art.* The Warrior-Saint's cloak is gray-blue lined with purple, and the robe of the Princess is pink. On the breast-harness of the horse is the inscription: RAPHAEL. It is almost certain that this painting was commissioned by Guidobaldo d'Urbino to be sent to the King of England in exchange for the Order of the Garter with which he was decorated on April 23, 1506. This is confirmed by the fact that the Warrior-Saint wears on his left leg the golden ribbon with the inscription: HONI, first word of the well-known motto of the Order: "Honi Soit Qui Mal Y Pense." In addition, this painting is mentioned in the inventory of Henry VIII's paintings for the years 1542–7 and is also mentioned in the inventory of the paintings of Charles I, and was acquired by Cardinal Mazarin for £150 at the sale of the latter's collections. Following several owners it became the property of Catherine of Russia and later passed to the Hermitage; the work was sold (1931) to Paul Mellon for the sum of $747,000 and finally reached its present location. The panel is unanimously attributed to Raphael, Cavalcaselle connecting it with the relief on the same theme executed by Donatello in Or San Michele in

Florence, and dating it towards the end of 1505 or beginning of 1506. This theory is accepted by, among others, Gamba, Ortolani, Carli, Longhi (1955), and Volpe, who narrows the date down to the early months of 1506; Fischel, Suida, and others favor 1504-5. The work was perhaps cleaned too thoroughly with a consequent loss of the patina in some parts; there are also traces of inexpert restoration.

Plate 63

MADONNA OF THE GOLDFINCH. *Panel, 107 × 77. Florence, Uffizi.* Mary, wearing a red robe under a blue cloak is depicted watching young St John, who offers Jesus the bird from which the work takes its title. Vasari notes that the work was painted for Vincenzo Nasi; in November 1547 (but on November 12, and not on November 17, as the biographer maintains) it was damaged when the Nasi Rome collapsed, restoration was consequently necessary; according to Gamba, it was entrusted to Michele di Ridolfo del Ghirlandaio. Several vertical cracks, clumsy repaints, and a general yellowing of the colors are still noticeable. In 1666 the panel became part of Cardinal Carlo de' Medici's Collection in the Uffizi. Critics are almost unanimous in dating it 1506. Three old copies are notable: one, once in the possession of Marchese Campana, in Geneva; another in 1835 in the English Verity Collection and then in the Victoria and Albert Museum, London; the third, at one time in the Hall of the Florentine Council of State where it arrived from the Sacristy of Vallombrosa.

Plate 64

MADONNA OF THE GOLDFINCH. Detail of the landscape at left.

Color Plate IV

THE DEPOSITION. Detail of plates 72-3, showing Nicodemus and the fainting Mary.

Plate 65

MADONNA OF THE GOLDFINCH. Detail of the landscape at right.

Plate 66

MADONNA OF THE GOLDFINCH. Detail of Mary's left hand.

Plate 67

MADONNA OF THE MEADOWS. *Panel, 113 × 88. Vienna, Kunsthistorisches Museum.* The landscape reminded Cavalcaselle of the surroundings of Passignano on Lake Trasimeno near Perugia. The date, M.D.VI, is inscribed along the golden edge of Mary's robe. It is unanimously identified as one of the two panels which, according to Vasari, Raphael painted in Florence for Taddeo Taddei, and which Vasari saw in Taddei's house. Baldinucci (*Notizie . . .*, Florence, 1681) notes that it was sold by the Taddei family to Archduke Ferdinand of Austria; it remained until 1663 in the Archduke's palace at Innsbruck, and was later transferred to the Castle of Ambras in the Tyrol. In 1773 it became part of the Imperial Viennese Collection and acquired the title, *Madonna del Belvedere* from its new location. In spite of the inscribed date many scholars date it 1505 (Gronau, Berenson, Fischel, Suida, and others), a year one may accept for the beginning of the work, though the whole must have been completed in 1506. The panel is well preserved. A copy exists in the Church of San Tommaso in Verona.

Plate 68

PORTRAIT OF ANGELO DONI. *Panel, 63 × 45. Florence, Pitti Palace.*

Born in 1476, Doni married Maddalena Strozzi in 1503 and commissioned portraits of his wife and
himself from Raphael. These portraits
were bequeathed to his heirs, whose
property they remained until 1826.
In this year they were sold for 2,500
sequins to Grand Duke Leopold II
of Tuscany, who bequeathed them
to the Pitti. This portrait is usually
dated 1506 or round that year.
Fischel favors 1505, but this date is
possibly too early. Cavalcaselle
thought it painted after *Maddalena
Doni*, but in fact it was painted
before, as was established by A.
Venturi. This is now almost unanimously accepted, particularly after
valid confirmation by M. Marangoni
(*La galleria Pitti*, Milan, 1951). On
the reverse of the panel a mediocre
follower of Raphael painted a monochrome picture of the myth of Deucalion and Pyrrha; the chronological
precedence of this theme when com-
pared with that represented on the
twin painting could be further proof
of the order in which these works
were painted. The panel is fairly well
preserved, except for some minor
repaints and a slight loss of patina.

Plate 69

PORTRAIT OF ANGELO DONI.
Detail of the hands.

Plate 70

PORTRAIT OF MADDALENA DONI.
Panel, 63 × 45. Florence, Pitti Palace.
Maddalena di Giovanni Strozzi was
born in 1489 and married Angelo
Doni in 1503. Her portrait and that
of her husband share the same
history (see comment on plate 68).
Ortolani believes that the sitter here
is not the wife of Doni, but his
mother-in-law, and considers that
Maddalena is portrayed in the
Portrait of a Young Woman in the

Borghese Gallery (plate 61). His
theory, however, has not been
accepted. Certainly the similarity of
landscapes and dimensions, and
monochrome pictures on the reverse
of both panels contradict this theory
(the monochrome executed here
depicts Deucalion and Pyrrha seeking
refuge). Nevertheless, one cannot
definitely maintain that the portrait
of Angelo was painted before that of
his wife. The panel is well preserved
except for minor repainting on the
forehead.

Plate 71

LA GRAVIDA (THE PREGNANT
WOMAN). *Panel, 66 × 52. Florence,
Pitti Palace.* Portrait of an unknown
woman in Florentine costume of the
beginning of the sixteenth century.
The bodice is orange, banded with
black, and the sleeves red with white
slashes. Filippini (*Cronache d'Arte*,
1925) identified the sitter as Emilia
Pia di Montefeltro, partly because
C. Ricci thought that this was the
pendant to the *Mute Woman* (plate
93), but this theory was never
accepted. The work is mentioned for
the first time at the beginning of the
eighteenth century in an inventory
of the Pitti, and is here ascribed to
an unknown artist. This attribution
lasted until Masselli (*La galleria
Pitti . . .*, 1839) suggested Raphael;
Passavant accepted the attribution,
with the date 1507; Cavalcaselle
thought it a work by Ridolfo del
Ghirlandaio; Morelli (1897) confirmed Masselli's hypothesis but set
the date two years earlier than
Passavant. All later critics have
accepted the attribution to Raphael,
Fischel dating it about 1505, Ortolani
1506, and Longhi 1505–6. The dark
background probably underwent
heavy over-painting which has not
altered the work's original appearance.

Plate 72–3

THE DEPOSITION. *Panel, 184* × *176. Rome, Borghese Gallery.* The panel bears the inscription: RAPHAEL VRBINAS M.D.VII low to the left of the step. The dead Christ is carried by two bearers (the one on the right is identified as Nicodemus); St John the Evangelist, St James (or Joseph of Arimathea), and Mary Magdalen are seen in the space between them; on the right behind them pious women support the fainting Mary. This work is connected with one of the most dramatic events in the history of Perugia: during the night of July 14, 1500, young Grifonetto Baglioni, with some accomplices, murdered four members of his own family who had been opposing his attempt to seize power in the town. One of those who escaped from the massacre, Giampaolo Baglioni, returned to Perugia two days later and killed Grifonetto; the latter's mother, Atalanta Baglioni, in memory of her intense grief, commissioned this panel from Raphael for the family chapel in the Church of San Francesco al Prato in Perugia. The painting remained in the Chapel until 1608, when it was secretly removed by the *frati minori conventuali* and sent to Pope Paul V in Rome; the latter made a present of it to his nephew, Scipione Borghese. The citizens of Perugia protested to their Cardinal, whose written reply merely stated that the painting was a private thing and that its sole owner was the Pope. To compensate them, however, for their loss, he presented them with a copy painted by Cavalier d'Arpino. In 1787, the original panel was carried off by the French and only returned to Rome in 1815. At least sixteen preparatory drawings, scattered between Oxford, London, Paris, and Florence, prove the elaborate concept of the work,

initially conceived as a *Lament over the Dead Christ*. Cavalcaselle, together with Ragghianti and others, noticed traces of co-operation (perhaps by Alfani). There are copies in museums in Turin and Perugia, where the secondary parts of the original whole are also to be found, the predella is in the Vatican (plates 82a–c).

Plate 74

THE DEPOSITION. Detail of the Christ's head.

Plate 75

THE DEPOSITION. Detail of the kneeling Mary.

Plate 76

THE DEPOSITION. Detail of the center.

Plate 77

THE CANIGIANI HOLY FAMILY. *Panel, 132* × *98. Munich, Alte Pinakothek.* St Elizabeth, wearing a blue cloak, red robe, and white head-cloth, holds young St John, whose attention is on Jesus seated on Mary's knees and holding a scroll inscribed: ECCE AGNUS DEI. The Virgin's robes are lead-red in tone; Joseph stands behind the group. Gamba believes that the background was inspired by a Northern print. On the neckband of Mary's dress is the inscription: RAPHAEL. VRBINAS. This work was painted for Domenico Canigiani of Florence, and is mentioned by Vasari as being the property of the former's heirs. One does not know how the panel came to the Medici family, but it is listed in the Uffizi inventory for the years 1589–1634. Through Anna Maria Luisa, daughter of the Grand Duke of Tuscany, Cosimo III, the work came into the possession of her husband, the Elector John William of Palatinate, who reserved it for his own gallery in Düsseldorf. In 1801, to hide it from the French, it was transferred to Munich. Dated by Fischel 1505–7, it seems plausible to date it 1507 or thereabouts (Gamba favors *c.* 1508) agreeing with most critics. Because of serious damage, the upper part was repainted in the eighteenth century, but at the beginning of the following century the repaints were partly removed. A copy by the School of Raphael was acquired by the Corsini Gallery, in Florence, from the Rinuccini Collection. Inscribed on the hem of the Virgin's dress in the copy are the letters: RAPHAEL.VRBINAS.INV., followed by some now defaced letters: SOLVTV . . ./CADEN . . ./PHV . . . In the sky are five angels to the left and three to the right; other noticeable variations are to be found in the landscape which "looks like a Flemish work" (Cavalcaselle). Another copy, even more different

and rather mediocre, is in the Urbino Gallery. According to Von Reber (*Catalogue. . . , de la Pinacothèque Royale de Munich*, Munich, 1885), the original also depicted a group of angels in the sky; this group had been partly removed by a band across the panel and partly covered by color when the work reached Düsseldorf.

Plate 78

THE CANIGIANI HOLY FAMILY. Detail of the landscape on the right.

Plate 79

THE CANIGIANI HOLY FAMILY. Detail of the landscape on the left.

Plate 80

THE CANIGIANI HOLY FAMILY. Detail of Joseph.

LOCATION OF PAINTINGS

BALTIMORE

WALTERS GALLERY

Madonna of the Candelabra (plate 150B; attribution).

EPSTEIN COLLECTION

Emilia Pia of Montefeltro (plate 35).

BERGAMO

ACCADEMIA CARRARA

St Sebastian (plate 5).

BERLIN

STAATLICHE MUSEEN

The Solly Madonna (plate 6).
Madonna with Child and SS Jerome and Francis (plate 7).
The Diotallevi Madonna (plate 28).
The Terranuova Madonna (plate 30).
The Colonna Madonna (plate 85).

BOLOGNA

PINACOTECA NAZIONALE

St Cecilia (plate 106).

BOSTON

ISABELLA STEWART GARDNER MUSEUM

Pietà (plate 40–41B).
Portrait of Fedra Inghirami (plate 112).

BRESCIA

PINACOTECA TOSIO MARTINENGO

Angel (plate 3).
Christ Blessing (plate 59).

BUDAPEST

MUSEUM OF FINE ARTS

Portrait of a Young Man (plate 29).
The Esterhazy Madonna (plate 55).

CHANTILLY

MUSÉE CONDÉ

The Three Graces (plate 45).
The Orléans Madonna (plate 56).

CITTÀ DI CASTELLO

PINACOTECA COMUNALE

Crucifixion (plate 1).
The Madonna of the Misericordia (plate 2).
Standard: Trinity with SS Sebastian and Roche, and *The Creation of Eve* (plate 9).

CRACOW

CZARTORYSKI MUSEUM

Portrait of a Young Man (plate 122B).

DRESDEN

GEMÄLDEGALERIE

The Sistine Madonna (plates 116, 117, and 118).

DULWICH (London)

COLLEGE GALLERY

A Franciscan Saint (plate 39A).
St Anthony of Padua (plate 39B).

FANO

CHURCH OF SANTA MARIA NUOVA

Nativity of the Virgin (plate 145; attribution).

FLORENCE

GALLERIA DELL'ACCADEMIA

Young St John (plate 151B; attribution).

UFFIZI

Portrait of Elisabetta Gonzaga (plate 34).
Young Man with an Apple (plate 36).
Self-portrait (plate 60).
Madonna of the Goldfinch (plates 63, 64, 65, and 66).
Portrait of Guidobaldo di Montefeltro (plate 92).
Portrait of Julius II (plate 104).
Leo X and Two Cardinals (plates 128 and color plate VIII, Part 2).
Portrait of a Man (plate 149A; attribution).

PITTI PALACE

The Granduca Madonna (plate 42).
Portrait of Angelo Doni (plates 68, 69).
Portrait of Maddalena Doni (plate 70).
La Gravida (plate 71).
The Madonna of the Canopy (plate 91).
The Madonna dell'Impannata (plate 109).
The Madonna of the Chair (plate 111).
Portrait of Fedra Inghirami (plate 113).
La Velata (plates 119, 120 and color plate VII, Part 2).
Portrait of Cardinal Bibbiena (plate 122A).

The Vision of Ezechiel (plates 125, 126, and 127).
Portrait of Julius II (plate 149B; attribution).

HAMPTON COURT

ROYAL GALLERY

Portrait of a Youth (plate 88).

HANOVER

LANDESGALERIE

The Veiled Woman (plate 33).

LENINGRAD

HERMITAGE

The Connestabile Madonna (plate 31).
Virgin and Child with Beardless St Joseph (plate 57).

LISBON

MUSEU NACIONAL DE ARTE ANTIGA

A Miracle of St Cyril (plate 14).

LONDON

NATIONAL GALLERY

The Mond Crucifixion (plates 10, 11, 12, 13, and color plate I, Part 1).
Ascent to Calvary (plate 40–41C).
Vision of a Knight (plate 44 and color plate II, Part 1).
The Ansidei Altarpiece (plates 49, 50, 51, 52, and color plate III, Part 1).
The Bridgewater Madonna (plate 84).
St Catherine of Alexandria (plates 89 and 90).
The Aldobrandini Madonna (plate 96 and color plate V, Part 2).

The Madonna of the Tower (plate 107).
Madonna and Child between SS Jerome and Francis (plate 148A; attribution).

ELLESMERE COLLECTION

Holy Family with Palm (plate 58).
Madonna in Landscape (plate 148B; attribution).

NORTHBROOK COLLECTION

The Northbrook Madonna (plate 54).

VICTORIA AND ALBERT MUSEUM

The Miraculous Draught of Fishes (plate 153A; cartoon).
The Delivery of the Keys (plate 153B; cartoon).
The Healing of the Lame Man (plate 155A; cartoon).
Elymas Struck with Blindness (plate 156A; cartoon).
The Death of Ananias (plate 157A; cartoon).
The Sacrifice at Lystra (plate 158A; cartoon).
The Preaching of St Paul (plate 159A; cartoon).

MADRID

THE PRADO

Holy Family with the Lamb (plate 83).
Portrait of a Cardinal (plates 98 and 99).
The Madonna of the Fish (plate 108 and color plate VI, Part 2).
The Spasimo di Sicilia (plate 124).
La Perla (plate 132).
Holy Family under the Oak (plate 133).
The Madonna of the Rose (plate 134).
The Visitation (plate 137).

MANTUA

PALAZZO DUCALE

Elymas Struck with Blindness (plate 156B; tapestry) and the other tapestries figuring in the Vatican series.

MILAN

BRERA GALLERY

The Marriage of the Virgin (plates 22, 23, 24, 25, 26, and 27).

MONTPELLIER

MUSÉE FABRE

Portrait of Lorenzo de' Medici (plate 144A; copy).

MUNICH

ALTE PINAKOTHEK

Self-portrait (plate 32).
The Canigiani Holy Family (plates 77, 78, 79, and 80).
The Casa Tempi Madonna (plate 95).
The Madonna of the Curtain (plate 110).

NAPLES

MUSEO NAZIONALE DI CAPODIMONTE

Portrait of a Cardinal (plate 105).
The Madonna of Divine Love (plate 135).
Mary and the Eternal Father with Cherubs (plate 146A; attribution).

NEW YORK

METROPOLITAN MUSEUM OF ART

The Colonna Altarpiece (plates 37 and 38).
The Agony in the Garden (plate 40–41A).
Portrait of Giuliano de' Medici (plate 150A; attribution).

OXFORD

ASHMOLEAN MUSEUM

Drawing for *The Deposition* (plate 81).

PARIS

THE LOUVRE

St Michael and the Demon (plates 46 and 47).
St George and the Dragon (plate 48).
La Belle Jardinière (plates 86 and 87).
The Madonna of the Veil (plate 103A).
The Diadem Madonna (plate 103B).
Portrait of Baldassar Castiglione (plates 114 and 115).
The Young St John (plate 121).
St Michael and the Devil (plate 129).
Holy Family of Francis I (plate 130).
Small Holy Family (plate 131).
Portrait of Giovanna of Aragon (plate 136).
Double Portrait (plate 138).
St Margaret (plate 151A; attribution).

PERUGIA

GALLERIA NAZIONALE DELL' UMBRIA

Ogee of *Flagellation* (plate 147B; attribution).

PHILADELPHIA

JOHNSON COLLECTION

Evangelist and Two Saints (plate 146B; attribution).

ROME

BORGHESE GALLERY

Portrait of a Man (plate 20).

Portrait of a Young Woman (plate 61).
The Deposition (plates 72–3, 74, 75, 76, and color plate IV, Part 1).
La Fornarina (plate 139).

DORIA GALLERY

Portrait of Andrea Navagero and Agostino Beazzano (plate 123).

PINACOTECA VATICANA

Coronation of the Virgin (plates 16, 17, 18, and 19).
The Christian Virtues (plates 82A-C).
The Foligno Madonna (plates 100, 101, and 102).
The Transfiguration (plates 140, 141, 142, and 143).
The Miraculous Draught of Fishes (plate 154A; tapestry).
The Delivery of the Keys (plate 154B; tapestry).
The Healing of the Lame Man (plate 155B; tapestry).
The Death of Ananias (plate 157B; tapestry).
The Sacrifice at Lystra (plate 158B; tapestry).
The Preaching of St Paul (plate 159B; tapestry).
The Stoning of St Stephen (plate 160A; tapestry).
The Conversion of St Paul (plate 160B; tapestry).

FORMERLY THE PROPERTY OF MARCHESE EMILIO VISCONTI VENOSTA

Crucifix with Saints (plate 8).

SÃO PAULO

ART MUSEUM

Resurrection (plate 4).

SUSSEX

Viscountess Mersey Collection

John the Baptist Preaching (plate 53).

Mrs Derek Fitzgerald Collection

The Miracle of St Jerome (plate 15).

URBINO

Galleria Nazionale delle Marche

La Muta (plate 93).

VADUZ (Liechtenstein)

Collection of the Prince

Portrait of a Gentleman (plate 21).

VIENNA

Kunsthistorisches Museum

Madonna of the Meadows (plate 67).
St Margaret (plate 144B; copy).

WASHINGTON

National Gallery of Art

The Small Cowper Madonna (plate 43).
St George and the Dragon (plate 62).
The Large Cowper Madonna (plate 94).
The Alba Madonna (plate 97).
The Flagellation (plate 147A; attribution).
Portrait of Bindo Altoviti (plate 152; attribution.

REPRODUCTIONS

ACKNOWLEDGEMENT FOR PLATES

Anderson, Rome: plates 3, 5, 9, 15–20, 22–26, 34, 36, 42, 59–61, 63, 68–76, 78, 83, 91, 93, 98–102, 104–6, 108, 109, 111, 113, 116–20, 122A, 123–5, 128, 132–5, 139–43, 147, 149, 151B, 155B, 157B, 158B, 159B, 160. *Alinari, Florence:* 45–48, 56, 86, 87, 103B, 115, 121, 129, 130, 136–8, 145, 151A, 154. *National Gallery, London:* 10–13, 40–41C, 44, 49–52, 89, 90, 96, 107, 148A. *Museu Nacional de Arte Antiga, Lisbon:* 14. *Kunstverlag Wolfrum, Vienna:* 21, 144B. *Calzolari, Mantua:* 156B. *Uffizi Gallery, Florence:* 64–66, 92, 126, 127. *Bayerische Staatsgemäldesammlungen, Munich:* 79–82, 110, 114. *Ministry of Works, London:* 88. *Braun, Paris:* 97. *Giraudon, Paris:* 103A. *Musée Fabre, Montpellier:* 144A. *Museo Nazionale di Capodimonte, Naples:* 146A. *John G. Johnson Art Collection, Philadelphia:* 146B. *Walters Gallery, Baltimore:* 150B. *Graphic Art Color, Milan:* 27. *Staatliche Museen, Berlin:* 28, 30. *Hanfstaengl, Munich:* 31. *Niedersächsische Landesgalerie, Hanover:* 33. *Epstein Collection, Baltimore:* 35. *Metropolitan Museum of Art, New York:* 37, 38, 40–41A, 150A. *Isabella Stewart Gardner Museum, Boston:* 40–41B, 112. *National Gallery of Art, Washington:* 43, 94. *Annan, Glasgow:* 58, 84, 148B. *Scala, Milan:* color plates IV (Part 1), II, III, IV (Part 2). *The remaining plates supplied by private sources.*

Plate I. CRUCIFIXION,
Città di Castello, Pinacoteca Comunale

Plate 2. THE MADONNA OF THE MISERICORDIA,
Citta di Castello, Pinacoteca Comunale

Plate 3. ANGEL,
Brescia, Pinacoteca Tosio Martinengo

Plate 4. RESURRECTION,
São Paulo, Art Museum

Plate 5. ST SEBASTIAN
Bergamo, Accademia Carrara

Plate 6. THE SOLLY MADONNA,
Berlin, Staatliche Museen

Plate 7. MADONNA WITH CHILD AND SS JEROME AND FRANCIS, Berlin, Staatliche Museen

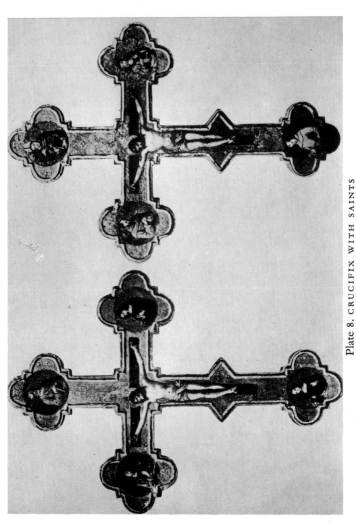

Plate 8. CRUCIFIX WITH SAINTS
Rome, formerly Marchese Emilio Visconti Venosta Collection

Plate 9. STANDARD,
Città di Castello, Pinacoteca Comunale

Plate 10. THE MOND CRUCIFIXION,
London, National Gallery

Plate 11. *Detail of plate 10*

Plate 12. *Detail of plate* 10

Plate 13. *Detail of plate* 10

Plate 14. A MIRACLE OF ST CYRIL,
Lisbon, Museu Nacional de Arte Antiga

Plate 15. THE MIRACLE OF ST JEROME,
Sussex, Mrs Derek Fitzgerald Collection

Plate 16. CORONATION OF THE VIRGIN,
Rome, Pinacoteca Vaticana

THE MOND CRUCIFIXION,
London, National Gallery
(*detail of plate 10*)

Plate 17. Predella of the CORONATION OF THE VIRGIN,
Rome, Pinacoteca Vaticana

Plate 18. *Detail of plate* 16

Plate 19. *Detail of plate* 16

Plate 20. PORTRAIT OF A MAN, Rome, Borghese Gallery

Plate 21. PORTRAIT OF A GENTLEMAN,
Vaduz, Collection of the Prince

Plate 22. THE MARRIAGE OF THE VIRGIN, Milan, Brera Gallery

Plate 23. *Detail of plate 22*

Plate 24. *Detail of plate 22*

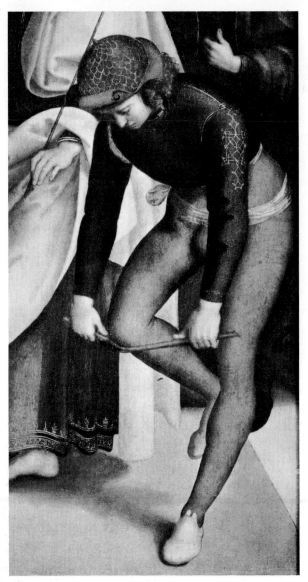

Plate 25. *Detail of plate 22*

Plate 26. *Detail of plate 22*

Plate 27. *Detail of plate 22*

Plate 28. THE DIOTALLEVI MADONNA,
Berlin, Staatliche Museen

Plate 29. PORTRAIT OF A YOUNG MAN,
Budapest, Museum of Fine Arts

Plate 30. THE TERRANUOVA MADONNA,
Berlin, Staatliche Museen

Plate 31. THE CONNESTABILE MADONNA,
Leningrad, Hermitage

Plate 32. SELF-PORTRAIT,
Munich, Alte Pinakothek

VISION OF A KNIGHT,
London, National Gallery
(*detail of plate 44*)

Plate 33. THE VEILED WOMAN, Hanover, Landesgalerie

Plate 34. PORTRAIT OF ELISABETTA GONZAGA, Florence, Uffizi

Plate 35. EMILIA PIA DI MONTEFELTRO, Baltimore, Epstein Collection

Plate 36. YOUNG MAN WITH AN APPLE,
Florence, Uffizi

Plate 37. THE COLONNA ALTARPIECE,
New York, Metropolitan Museum of Art

Plate 38. *Detail of plate 37*

Plate 39. A FRANCISCAN SAINT AND ST ANTHONY OF PADUA
Dulwich, College Gallery

Plate 40–1. Predella of THE
New York, B

COLONNA ALTARPIECE,
on, London

Plate 42. THE GRANDUCA MADONNA,
Florence, Pitti Palace

Plate 43. THE SMALL COWPER MADONNA,
Washington, National Gallery of Art

Plate 44. VISION OF A KNIGHT,
London, National Gallery

Plate 45. THE THREE GRACES,
Chantilly, Musée Condé

Plate 46. ST MICHAEL AND THE DEMON,
Paris, Louvre

Plate 47. *Detail of plate 46*

Plate 48. ST GEORGE AND THE DRAGON,
Paris, Louvre

THE ANSIDEI ALTARPIECE,
London, National Gallery
(*detail of plate 49*)

Plate 49. THE ANSIDEI ALTARPIECE,
London, National Gallery

Plate 50. *Detail of plate 49*

Plate 51. *Detail of plate* 49

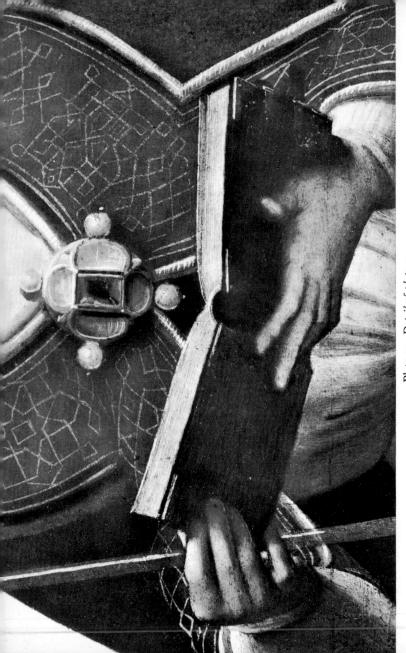

Plate 52. *Detail of plate 49*

Plate 53. Predella of THE ANSIDEI ALTARPIECE,
Sussex, Viscountess Mersey Collection

Plate 54. THE NORTHBROOK MADONNA,
London, Lord Northbrook Collection

Plate 55. THE ESTERHAZY MADONNA,
Budapest, Museum of Fine Arts

Plate 56. THE ORLÉANS MADONNA,
Chantilly, Musée Condé

Plate 57. VIRGIN AND CHILD WITH BEARDLESS ST JOSEPH,
Leningrad, Hermitage

Plate 58. HOLY FAMILY WITH PALM
London, Ellesmere Collection

Plate 59. CHRIST BLESSING,
Brescia, Pinacoteca Tosio Martinengo

Plate 60. SELF-PORTRAIT,
Florence, Uffizi

Plate 61. PORTRAIT OF A YOUNG WOMAN,
Rome, Borghese Gallery

Plate 62. ST GEORGE AND THE DRAGON
Washington, National Gallery of Art

Plate 63. MADONNA OF THE GOLDFINCH,
Florence, Uffizi

Plate 64. *Detail of plate 63.*

THE DEPOSITION,
Rome, Gallery Borghese
(*detail of plate 72–3*)

Plate 65. *Detail of plate 63*

Plate 66. *Detail of plate 63*

Plate 67. MADONNA OF THE MEADOWS,
Vienna, Kunsthistorisches Museum

Plate 68. PORTRAIT OF ANGELO DONI,
Florence, Pitti Palace

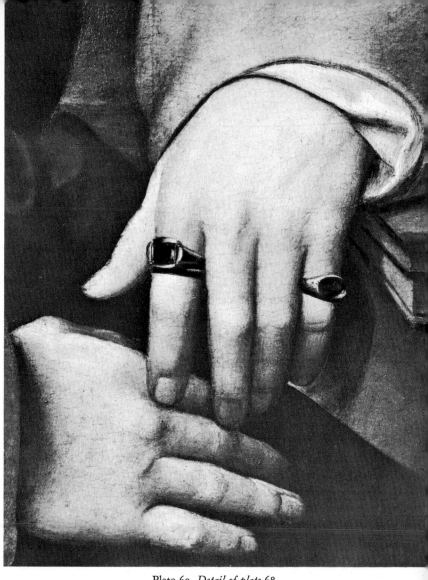

Plate 69. *Detail of plate 68*

Plate 70. PORTRAIT OF MADDALENA DONI,
Florence, Pitti Palace

Plate 71. LA GRAVIDA,
Florence, Pitti Palace

Plate 72–73 T
Rome, Bo

DEPOSITION,
ese Gallery

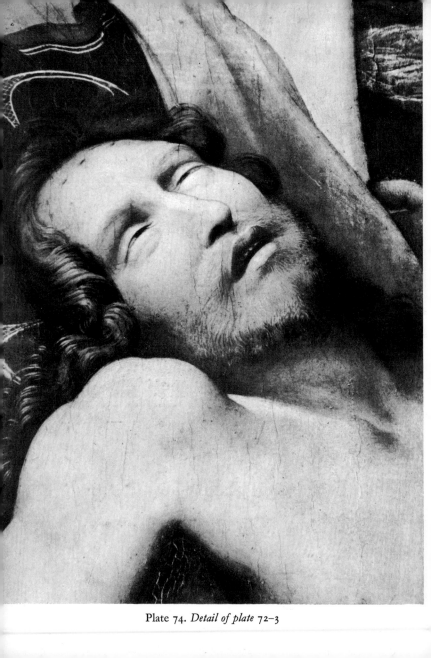

Plate 74. *Detail of plate 72–3*

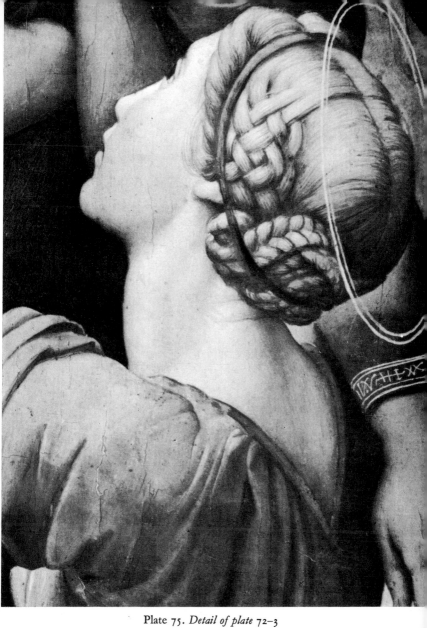

Plate 75. *Detail of plate* 72–3

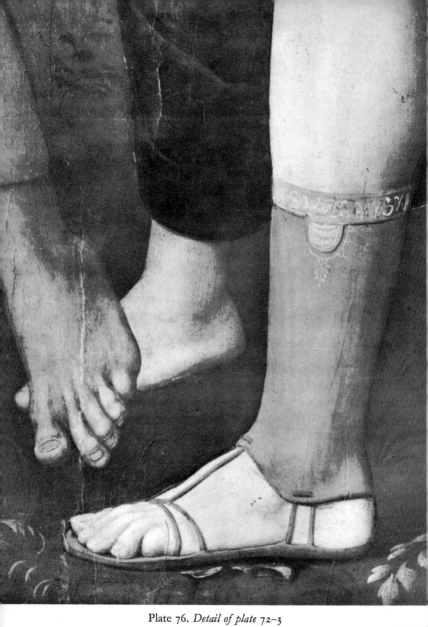

Plate 76. *Detail of plate 72–3*

Plate 77. THE CANIGIANI HOLY FAMILY,
Munich, Alte Pinakothek

Plate 78. *Detail of plate 77*

Plate 79. *Detail of plate* 77

Plate 80. *Detail of plate* 77

Plate 79. *Detail of plate* 77

Plate 80. *Detail of plate* 77